From Newport to Perth

THE LOUIS VUITTON CUP – THE AMERICA'S CUP

From Newport to Perth

THE NEW CHALLENGE

SHERIDAN HOUSE

This edition first published in the
United States of America 1986 by
Sheridan House Inc.
145 Palisade St. Dobbs Ferry, N.Y. 10522

Main texts by Margherita Bottini, Berkeley Crane and Bruce Stannard

Additional texts by Chris Freer, Ben Lexcen, John Marshall and Bruno Troublé.

Typeset by Inforum Ltd, Portsmouth UK

Printed in Italy

ISBN 0 911378 64 2

PHOTOGRAPHIC CREDITS

Beken of Cowes: pp. 8/9, 14/15 (top), 18, 21.
Borlenghi, Carlo: pp. 39, 44/45, 59 (right), 62/3, 120/121, 122, 123, 124/125.
Bottini, Margherita: pp. 30/31 (top), 32/33, 34/35, 36/37, 42/43, 50/51, 52, 54/58, 60/61, 66, 67, 68, 69, 70/71, 82/83, 84 (above), 85, 86/87, 88 (bottom), 104 (right), 106/107, 108/109, 112/113, 114/115, 116/117, 132/133, 136, 137, 138/139, 140/141, 142/143, 150/151, 153, 158, 162/163 (top), 168, 169 (bottom), 171 (bottom), 172/173.
Evans Koren/Kos Photos: pp. 92, 93, 94, 95, 96, 97, 98/99.
Garwood, Roger/Photomarine: pp. 148/149, 152, 154/155, 159, 160, 161, 163 (bottom), 164/165, 169 (top), 170/171 (top).
Green, Sharon/Windward Productions: pp. 128, 129, 130/131.
Humphris, Jane/Yachtshots: pp. 177, 178/179.
Levick Collection, Courtesy of the Mariner's Museum, Newport News, Virginia, USA: p. 20 (left).
Mystic Seaport Museum, Mystic, Connecticut, USA: p. 20 (right).
Nerney, Dan: pp. 22/23.
From *Paine Burgess Testimonial*, Boston, City Council, 1887: pp. 12, 13, 14/15 (bottom).
Plisson, Philip/Explorer-Overseas: pp. 102, 103, 104 (left), 105.
Pyle, Barbara: pp. 28, 29.
Rosenfeld, Stanley: p. 19.
Stannard, Bruce: p. 176.
Vegliani, Stefano: p. 84 (bottom).
Villarosa, Riccardo/Overseas: pp. 30 (bottom), 40/41.
P. Vilminot: p. 180.
Warner, Laurie/Photovation: 74, 75, 76, 77, 78/79, 88 (top), 89.

Contents

In 1861 the schooner America *won the Hundred Guinea Cup on English waters, getting the better of 14 English adversaries, much to the astonishment of Queen Victoria who was watching. 19 years later the same silver trophy, re-christened the America's Cup, was the coveted prize for the winner of a race held on the Hudson River.*

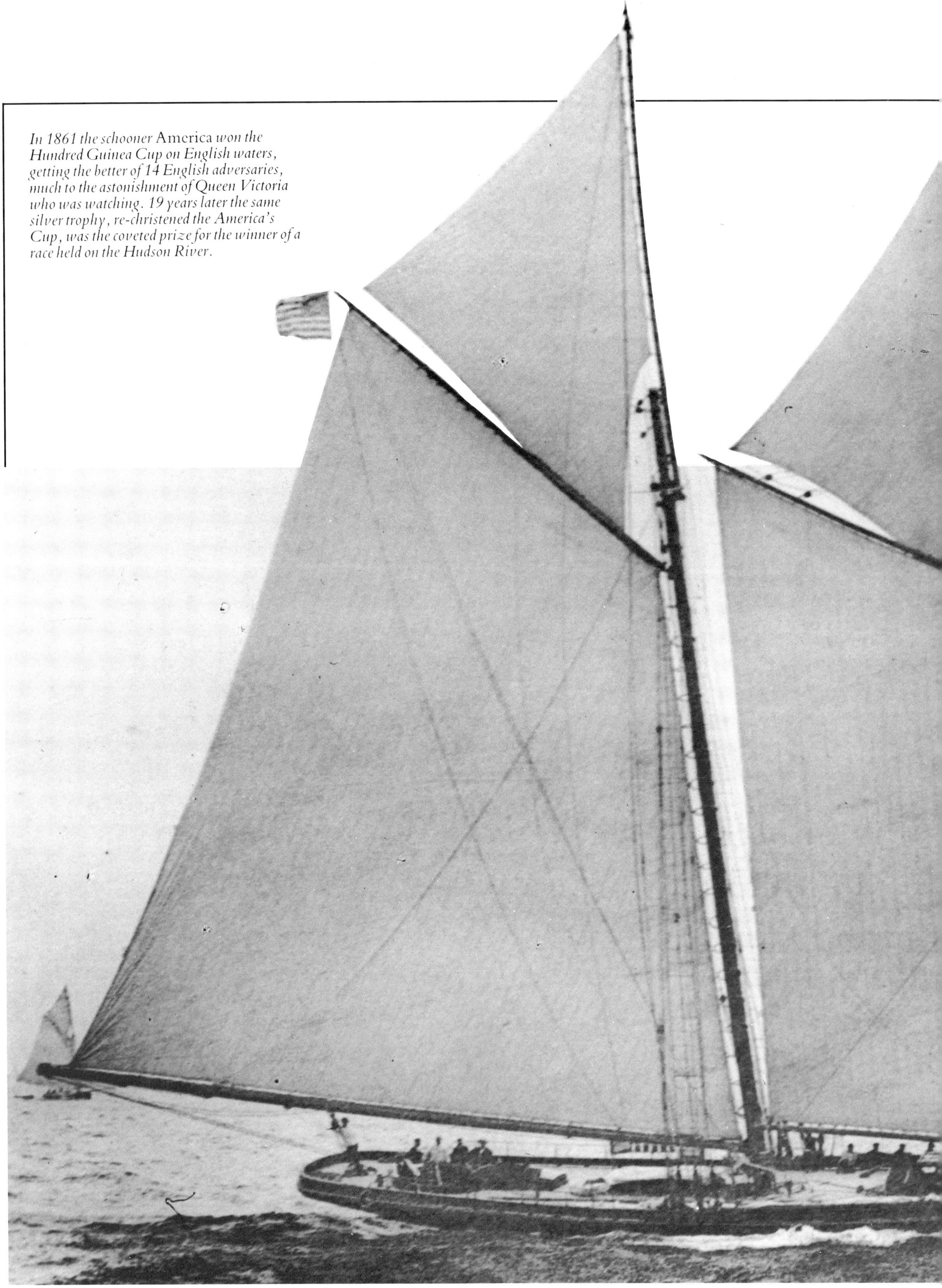

The History

1851

When London jeweller Robert Garrard decided to create a limited edition of three silver objects in the year 1848, he certainly could not have foreseen the great importance his decision was to eventually assume. The cups he created were of little artistic value and certainly of no functional value at all, since they were bottomless. The one example of this insignificant cup remained unsold, and waited quite some time before embarking on its true destiny.

In 1851, the Hundred Guineas Cup (the price of the cup at the time) became the prize offered by the Royal Yacht Squadron for a regatta 'around the Isle of Wight'. Won by the schooner *America*, the regatta marked the beginning of what was to become much more than a simple yacht race or tactical event. *America* became a symbol of man's exploitation of technology. She won the regatta, but not in a way that was any more remarkable than later yachts which won but which never acquired legendary status.

America was sent to England in 1851 by the New York Yacht Club; she had been specially designed by George Steers and was skippered by John Cox Stevens. She sailed in only two regattas during August that year, however, and despite having missed a lap of the course, and after the strongest competitors had been obliged to retire, *America* won the Hundred Guineas Cup. The regatta itself was held in real time, ie with no handicaps. Had it been held using the New York system of handicaps, *America* would have come in second.

The fact that *America* made history has more to do with her design rather than her successes. She was unlike the traditional English yachts of the time, for she had a streamlined, concave prow and machine-woven cotton sails (English sails were still hand-made at the time, and were made of linen). *America* showed the Old World what clippers were already doing on trade routes – giving unexpected performance.

'If the *America* is on the right course, then we are all on the wrong one . . .' These were the significant words with which the Marquis of Anglesey, a leading figure in British yachting, greeted the American schooner at Cowes. His words expressed the disbelief of the Establishment, suddenly confronted with new ideas and parameters. They were the same words that the incredulous Americans were to repeat so fatally in the year 1983, when confronted by *Australia II*.

In 1851, the British were obliged to admit that one of their former colonies, New England, had independently developed certain new and profitable ideas in boat design. Whereas English boats were being built ever deeper and narrower with straight bows (cutters), American boats were wider, flatter, lighter, and in many cases came with a centreboard. What made news during that summer was the first defeat for English yachting, a defeat which the newspapers made much of and the significance of which was magnified by the public itself. Other yachting pioneers followed the events in the English newspapers. In Sydney and Melbourne, the design of a 'type' of yacht and a 'formula' were the subjects of discussion. In 1856, they imported the first English yachts, *Mischief*, *Surprise* and *Presto*. *Mischief* was described as 'the first yacht showing the influence of *America* on English boat design in Sydney Bay.'

In 1862, the Royal Sydney Yacht Squadron was founded, and in 1865, the Royal Perth Yacht Club.

The success of *America* also started an era of international events not connected with the Cup.

Between 1851 and 1871, a total of 36 races were held between American and English yachts, 26 of which were won by the Americans (not always by very much of a margin, however). The ideas of boat designers and builders from both sides of the Atlantic began to influence each other more and more, and the same influence affected the rules of boat racing as well.

1887

In 1857, the members of the America Syndicate passed the Cup to the New York Yacht Club, to be offered as an international trophy. Eighteen clubs from all over the world were informed of the decision. This was how the Deed of Gift originated: the act of offering a prize which is the basis of every competition. This deed contained the rules of the race as well, and had to be modified several times through the history of yachting; its interpretation has often led to bitter disputes between competitors. The uniqueness of the America's Cup lies in the regulations as well; one item established by the Deed of Gift is the size of the hull, plus the fact that it must be designed and built in the entrant's country – a unique clause in the world of regattas.

In 1868, another American schooner, *Sappho*, raced in the Solent. It is said that the result of this race led the English to make the first challenge in 1870, with James Ashbury and the schooner *Cambria*, designed by Ratsey. This challenge involved the first east to west transatlantic race, for the *Cambria* raced the American schooner *Dauntless* over to America. Cambria was to win that race, but she came in only tenth in the Cup itself. The Americans returned the hospitality they had received at Cowes 19 years previously by entering a fleet of 14 adversaries.

A small scooner called *Magic*, designed by Looper, won in extra time. Ashbury renewed the challenge in 1871 with *Livonia*, designed by Woods along American lines. Ashbury won in only one of six regattas against a single adversary at a time. This was to herald the birth of match racing with two competitors only, another element of the America's Cup.

In 1871, the New York Yacht Club still reserved the right to choose the defender from among four yachts, on a day-by-day basis. The club was thus represented in three heats by *Columbia* and in two others by *Sappho* (which had had some improvements made since 1868). Ashbury won only one heat – the third – but registered an official complaint about the second one and requested it to be held again. He also requested the sixth heat in the programme to be sailed. Public opinion was on his side, but the New York Yacht Club would not accept his protest and closed the race with the score at four to one. The English, naturally enough, took Ashbury's side, and the resulting bad feeling took a long time to die down.

The next America's Cup was held in 1876, and in 1881 two Canadian entrants took part. In order to avoid further disputes, the New York Yacht Club ruled that the competition was to be based on three heats, with the nomination of a single defending yacht. Holding the race at Newport, one of the Club's obligatory stop-overs in its own annual event, was also given some consideration. In the end, however, the waters of Staten Island and Sandy Hook were chosen again. It was the last challenge in which only two schooners took part: the Canadian *Countess of Dufferin* was the challenger, designed and built by Alexander Cuthberth; the defender was *Madeleine*, an older centreboard schooner designed by Kirby. In 1881, Cuthberth brought *Atlanta* to New York, and on this occasion the New York Yacht Club organized selection heats for the first time, in order to nominate the defender. Three sloops took part and *Mischief*, designed by Cary Smith, won. In the same year a small Scottish cutter named *Madge* outclassed all the American boats of her size in the New York waters. On the other side of the Atlantic long, deep and narrow cutters continued to be successful. Two typical versions of this kind of boat were *Genesta* and *Galatea*, the latter built of steel and designed by Beavor Webb; both were challengers in 1885 and 1886 respectively. The defenders were *Puritan* and *Mayflower*, designed by Edward Burgess, who came up with a boat halfway between the two schools of thought – the 'compromise' cutter. For the first time, boat design from both sides of the Atlantic began to merge.

ABOVE: Genesta, *the English cutter belonging to Sir Richard Sutton and designed by J Beavor-Webb.* LEFT: *Men at work on the bowsprit of* Puritan, *the Eastern Yacht Club's boat designed by Edward Burgess.*

FAR RIGHT, above: Galatea, *the English sloop defeated in 1886, surrounded by spectator craft*. BELOW, far right: Thistle, *the Scottish challenger in 1887;* left, Volunteer, *designed by George Watson, was captained by John Barr, brother of the more famous Charlie, skipper of numerous victorious defenders.*

1887

The Americans continued to dominate the America's Cup, even though their yachts were not always proven unbeatable. The truth of the matter was that they started out with clear advantages. They sailed on home waters, whereas the challengers were obliged to sail their boats to New York. Furthermore, ever since the first race, the Americans had established a method of preparation which was largely financed by syndicates made up of major industrialists and financiers, and which involved two months of selection trials.

In America in 1883, and soon afterwards in England, a new classification system was introduced. It was based on the length at the waterline and on the sail area; a formula favouring the longer overall lengths with large rakes and long overhangs. The last 20 years of the nineteenth century were dominated by fin keels. This period also heralded the introduction of the concept of the racing boat with limited accommodation.

Australia was also designing and building racing yachts. The first all-Australian yacht was built in 1858, designed by Dick Narnett and named *Australian*. It was a most radical design for the time. In 1888, Walter Reeks, the most famous yacht designer in Sydney went to America 'to inspect American yachts with the idea of building an Australian one with which to challenge the New York Yacht Club'. The idea seems quite extraordinary when one considers that the Australians could only reach New York via Cape Horn or the Indian Ocean, and had to do so in a regatta boat in which the hull at the waterline would be no longer than about 90 feet, a regulation brought in that year. Reeks's idea of getting a group of financiers interested in the Royal Sydney Yacht Squadron challenge did not materialize, and he was forced to abandon the project. It was not to be reconsidered by the Australians until 1958.

England and America continued to share their experiences. A 'compromise' cutter, *Volunteer* (designed by Edward Burgess) defended the Cup in 1887. This time the beaten challenger was a design by George Watson. He had designed *Thistle*, a deep, narrow boat which was lighter than its predecessors: she had a raked prow and poop, and the centreboard was separate from the actual hull. The straight stem of the English cutter had disappeared forever.

At the same time, a great innovator had appeared on the American scene. His name was Nat Herreshoff, and his boats were to defend the Cup six times. He made his name with *Gloriana*, which was too small to sail for the Cup, but which nevertheless made sailing history during those years. She had massive rakes and the lowest possible central weighting. She pitched less than her competitors, and her extreme stability was so perfect that amazed observers could not understand how it came about. Herreshoff also constructed the boat in steel, and sheathed it with wood. He built *Colonia* in steel for the 1893 challenge, and also *Vigilant* with a hull in polished bronze and a centreboard. *Vigilant* dominated the heats and beat the challenger *Valkyrie*, another boat designed by George Watson. Herreshoff continued his research into the use of new materials and construction techniques. For *Defender* (1895), he made the hull in bronze with a cover of aluminium. The materials set off electrolysis and were therefore subject to corrosion. The vessel was not destined to last for long but the Cup was saved! In 1899, Sir Thomas Lipton entered the scene. He was to challenge for the Cup five times, with five versions of *Shamrock*.

In 1899, Newport was discussed once again as a venue. It was the Gilded Age, the era in which the Rhode Island resident dedicated his life to earthly pleasures. Great industrialists and financiers built themselves so-called country cottages there. In reality, they were residences on a princely scale.

It was in Newport that the New York Yacht Club took up summer residence in 1892. In 1899, Rhode Island Sound was chosen for holding the trials to select the defender and *Columbia*, with a steel mast,

1938

dominated the season. The battle between Lipton and the New York Yacht Club continued. In 1901, *Shamrock II* competed. Designed by Watson, she was beaten by the very same *Columbia* which had been the leading light the year before. In 1903, *Shamrock III*, designed by William Fife, was beaten by *Reliance*, considered at the time as being the most extreme example of the hull formula then in use. *Reliance* was enormous and was the largest single-masted racing yacht ever built. She was 144 feet LOA and carried a sail area of 16,159 square feet. She lasted only one season, however, and it is said that she cost $450,000, a fortune at the time. But bear in mind that the head of the financing committee was none other than Cornelius Vanderbilt, a man who had built himself a neo-classical residence, The Brakers, containing 70 rooms!

Meanwhile, the tendency to build increasingly extreme, empty, light boats had generated a reaction. The Americans brought in the Universal Rule in 1901, researched by Herreshoff himself. This new formula favoured heavier boats which were subdivided into classes classified by letters. The era of the J-Class had begun. Europe followed suit in 1906 with the same formula, and the Metre classes were born. The Universal Rule was also applied in Australia, where match racing was being developed with the Sayonara Cup competition, begun in 1904, and followed shortly afterwards by the Northcote Cup.

In 1920, *Shamrock IV* was beaten by *Resolute*, but ever since 1912, Lipton had proposed changing over to the J-Class and racing in real time. His proposal was accepted for the first challenge which took place after the First World War – in 1920, to be exact, when the entire Cup event was transferred to Newport. The J-Class boats were 75 feet long on the waterline and were the boats that fought for the Cup in 1930, 1934, and 1937. The Cup was defended by Harold Vanderbilt at all three events, with boats designed by Starling Burgess: *Enterprise, Rainbow*, and *Ranger*, which respectively beat Lipton's last *Shamrock*, designed by Nicholson, and Tom Sopwith's two *Endeavours* (the latter two designed by Nicholson as well). The first proved to be decidedly superior to the defender, and Nicholson, in a very sporting gesture, offered the plans to Burgess. Like *America* and *Reliance*, *Ranger* was destined to pass into yachting history. She was designed by a team under the direction of Burgess, and Olin Stephens helped with the research. For the first time, the testing of scale models in ship model basins was discussed seriously. Kenneth Davidson carried out the *Ranger* tests at the Stevens Institute. While the J-Class boat represented the image of the era, the classes resulting from the Universal Rule, which were much smaller and cheaper, created quite a new image. With the 6-, 8- and 12-Metre classes as laid down by Universal Rule, yachting broadened its horizons. Another contribution to this widening field was the development of ocean racing. The 1931 Newport-Plymouth transatlantic race in which *Dorade* appeared, brought to light the names of two brothers – Rod and Olin Stephens. Olin, who worked in the Sparkman & Stephens workshop in New York, had collaborated on the building of *Ranger*. He had designed another two boats that are considered fundamental in the history of modern yacht design: the 6-Metre *Goose* and the 12-Metre *Vim*, which after being tested in a ship model basin were taken to race in England in 1939 by Harold Vanderbilt. Competition in England in this class was particularly fierce at the time. *Vim* won a total of 14 regattas, a result which probably impressed the English even more than the Americans.

12-Metre yachts had already appeared in the New York events in 1928 and were considered 'relatively simple boats with good ability, and capable of ocean sailing'. The America's Cup was destined, however, to become the specialized race purely for regatta boats.

ABOVE: Vigilant, *victorious defender in 1893 due to her sliding keel, was the first of a long series of defenders designed by Nat Herreshoff.* OPPOSITE: Columbia *and* Shamrock II, *running on different tacks in the 1901 Cup challenge.*

LEFT: *Up* Ranger*'s mast. On the left, Rod Stephens, who had the habit of climbing all over the place to make technical check-ups.* ABOVE: *Nathanael Herreshoff who, between 1893 and 1920, designed six winning defenders.* OPPOSITE: Endeavour II, *despite her professional crew, failed to win even one race.* OVERLEAF: Courageous, *the 12-Metre with which Ted Turner beat Australia in 1977.*

J
K6

12-Metres

1958

The modern era for the America's Cup began in 1958. The Deed of Gift was extended to include the 12-Metre Class; the minimum waterline length was brought up to 44 feet (a little over 19 metres), and the challenger was no longer required to reach New York in his own boat. Several times during the 12-Metre era, the basin tests produced questionable results. The results of the tests carried out by the English on *Sceptre* did not correspond with the real capabilities of the boat, and so Stephen's *Columbia* defended the Cup with ease in 1958, after having beaten the old-fashioned *Vim* in the trials as well as Ray Hunt's *Easterner* and Phil Rhodes's *Weatherly*.

In 1962, *Columbia* and *Easterner* participated again in the American selection heats together with the new *Nefertiti* designed by Ted Hood, but it was the old and modified *Weatherly*, skippered by Bus Mosbacher, which won the selections and successfully defended the Cup. At this point the New York Yacht Club decided to hold not more than one match every three years, and examined the idea of holding selection trials between the challengers. It was also established that, apart from the hulls, the sails and fittings should be made in the same country as the club taking part, and limitations were also placed on the use of research institutes and model basins. What it did, in fact, was prevent challenging clubs from using the Stevens Institute facilities. In 1964, the challenge made by the Royal Thames Yacht Club was accepted. Two groups built two 12-Metre boats designed by David Boyd, *Sovereign* and *Kurrewa V*. *Sovereign* competed against the Cup defender, *Constellation*, another Sparkman & Stephens design. It was Stephens too who supplied the 1967 defender, *Intrepid*, which opened the way to the modern conception of a 12-Metre boat. Stephens, in fact, separated the rudder from the keel fin and inserted a second rudder, the trim tab, into the poop part of the fin itself. This reduced the underwater surface and increased manouevrability. In 1966, while he was carrying out the research for *Intrepid* at the Stephens Institute, Olin Stephens tested a type of keel not unlike the winged keel, which was to be adopted on *Australia II*. Skippered by Mosbacher, *Intrepid* beat the second Australian challenger *Dame Pattie*, skippered by Jock Sturrock.

In 1970, two challenges were accepted, one from Australia and one from France. For the first time in the history of the Cup, the challengers raced selection trials. *Gretel*, an Alan Payne design, skippered by Jim Hardy, beat *France*. Payne's boat was decidedly superior to Baron Bich's *France*, designed by André Mauric. The American defender was *Intrepid* once again, substantially modified by Britton Chance and skippered by Bill Ficker.

The 1973 challenge was postponed until a year later, in order to leave time for the adoption of a new material, aluminium, which ended the era of the wooden hull.

After the defeat of *Valiant* in 1970, the Sparkman & Stephens workshop designed *Courageous* and the Britton Chance *Mariner* for the 1974 Cup. Both were in aluminium, and *Mariner* included radical changes which gave promising results in the model basin. She was, however, to prove very slow in reality.

In 1974, the selection trials between the challengers again saw the French and Australians with the first Alan Bond boat designed by Bob Lexcen (then known as Bob Miller). His first 12-Metre boat was *Southern Cross*, and the Australians easily beat *France*. *Courageous* defended the Cup with a clear four to one win. Ted Hood was the skipper and Dennis Conner the starting helmsman. It was not only the undoubtable capability of the Sparkman & Stephens workshop which determined American superiority, but also the sails they used.

Courageous again defended the Cup in 1977 against *Australia*; it was Lexcen's second 12-Metre boat (with John Valentijn as assistant). In the trials to select the defender, the candidates were *Courageous*, *Enterprise* and *Independence*. The challengers were

1983

Australia, Pelle Petterson's *Sverige*, and André Mauric's *France II*. The result was again four to one to the Americans.

In 1980, Alan Bond took back the same *Australia* to Newport, but Jim Hardy was the skipper and John Bertrand the sail trimmer. The *Freedom* Syndicate dominated the American entrants. Its skipper, Dennis Conner, changed the entire approach to the Cup. What he did was to make it a full-time job with the constant support of a sparring partner – in this case, *Enterprise*. *Freedom* was yet another project from the Sparkman & Stephens workshop.

There were three challengers apart from *Australia: France III, Sverige*, and the English *Lionheart*, and it was an English invention which distinguished the 1980 Cup. *Lionheart*, designed by Ian Howlett, was fitted with a bendy rig, which the Australians adopted for the finals against *Freedom*, in which they managed to win one race. Then, beaten again, they dedicated themselves to creating what was to be their super boat for 1983. John Bertrand was immediately named skipper, no old trial horse was acquired, and even *Australia* was sold to the English.

The Italians challenged for the Cup for the first time in 1983, the French returned along with the English and Canadians, and the Australians and Americans entered three boats. The first boat, designed by Dave Pedrick, was skippered by Tom Blackaller; the second, the remodified *Courageous*, was skippered by John Kolius. However, the *Freedom* Syndicate had the most funds available, and Dennis Conner's team began to build three boats. In 1982, *Spirit of America*, designed by the Sparkman & Stephens workshop and *Magic*, designed by John Valentijn, were launched, but neither performed better than the trial horse *Freedom*. Having tried to persuade both designers to work with them, Conner's team therefore turned the project for the third boat over to Valtijn. This created quite a stir, and the Sparkman & Stephens workshop concentrated on refitting *Courageous*. Conner asked Valentijn to develop *Freedom*, and the result was *Liberty*. Meanwhile, Ben Lexcen developed the idea of the winged keel.

The summer of 1983 was full of surprises. Newport had never seen such a huge fleet of 12-Metre boats: *Advance, Australia II, Azzurra, Canada, Challenge 12, Victory '82* and *'83, France, Courageous, Defender, Freedom* and *Liberty*. *Australia II* dominated the selection trials and the Louis Vuitton Cup. The New York Yacht Club contested the legality of its new winged keel, which had been kept a secret up until then. The Australians were also competing at a psychological level, having decided not to reveal the underside of the *Australia II* until the last moment. This heralded the birth of the keel gate.

First the Americans objected to the potential nonconformity of the shape of the fin on *Australia II*, an unknown quantity to both them and to the Universal Rule. Then they criticized the legitimacy, in terms of nationality, of the team which had collaborated in its design. Had it wanted to, in theory the New York Yacht Club had the right to withdraw the Cup, being responsible for the correct application of the Deed of Gift. It was an institutional right which the America's Cup Committee preferred not to avail itself of, evidently for political reasons. The Club did not wish to face public reaction when it was already considered to be lacking in sporting spirit. So Conner and his team, already psychologically weakened, began the match of the century with their yacht *Liberty*. They doggedly defended themselves, and after two series were level at three races each, the Australians won the last race, and the Cup. For Bond, Bertrand and Lexcen, it was the crowning achievement of years of hard work. The chief achievement of the Australian team had been demonstrating that man's creativity, using the most advanced means of calculation and forecasting, can result in advanced and radical winning designs.

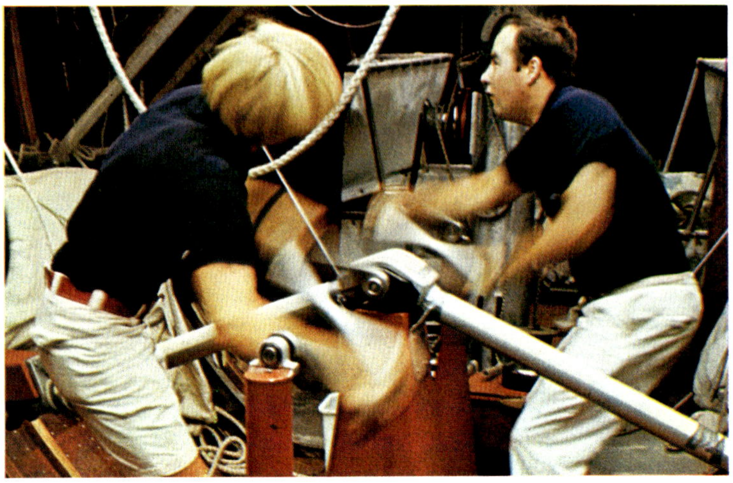

ABOVE: The crew of *Intrepid* in 1967 with Bus Mosbacher at the helm. LEFT: The crew of *Intrepid* trimming a sheet in 1970. Before 1977, winches could be set below decks, but the rule was changed for safety reasons. RIGHT: *Gretel II*, fitted with two wheels and skippered by Jim Hardy, was beaten by *Intrepid* in 1970.

GRETEL II
SYDNEY

ABOVE: Liberty *and her stablemate* Freedom *sailing back into harbour after an exercise race in 1983.* OPPOSITE: Australia II, *the yacht responsible for bringing to an end the American supremacy which had lasted 132 years.*

12
KA-6
KA-6

ABOVE: *Newport, 26th September 1983: the jubilation of the crew after the fourth victory of* Australia II. BELOW LEFT: *John Bertrand and financier Alan Bond (right) with the recently acquired Cup.* OVERLEAF: *façade of the Municipal Council building in Fremantle, the port which will receive the home-coming fleet in the 1986–87 America's Cup.*

From Newport to Perth

397
NICIPAL
COUNCIL
NEC PRETIO
ANTLE

5.20 pm on the 26th September 1983, off Rhode Island. Newport silently watches the end of a myth. The celebrations, the ovations, and the enthusiastic crowd will all come later, illuminated by hundreds of boats, when the winners and the vanquished, together with the spectators, will make for the port.

Newport's first reply to the inevitability of history is a surreal silence. Only at this moment does Newport really discover that it has no right to the America's Cup, a cup which, unlike other yachting events, has no fixed venue.

The news leaves people dumbfounded. There are those who say that the Cup should be melted down and made into an Australian salver, just as there are those who think the name should be changed to the Australia's Cup.

Upsetting the status quo that had lasted for over 100 years meant the beginning of a voyage towards the unknown. The public rushed off to their atlases to check where Perth was. The revelation about the amazing keel made technicians realize just how much was due to design. Designers were obliged to come up with an entirely new conception of the 12-Metre yacht. And what about the organizers? They had to solve logistic problems that had never been encountered before. Last of all, the crews were to be obliged to sail in far more demanding waters.

Newport remained silent, and the America's Cup prepared to face the unknown.

The scene changes. Gone are the meadows, the mansions, the old jetties and the fog. The horizon is now limpid, permeated with the colours of the Indian Ocean. The voyage towards Perth becomes a reality and Fremantle, the port of Perth, even more so.

The roles are now reversed. Everything seems possible to the new challengers; the Americans are not unbeatable and the vanquished have to lick their wounds.

Newport and its traditions seem a whole world away, and a new way of tackling the America's Cup comes into being. Attention shifts to the least-known state of this faraway continent: Western Australia. The comment from one crew member sailing on the Indian Ocean for the first time was as follows: 'That was a pretty trick Dennis Conner played on us all right, getting us into a godforsaken place like this. And wind, nothing but wind, with the boats likely to become submarines at any moment, filling up with water, and all of us soaked to the skin with seawater and salt . . .' Not only has the venue changed, but there is also another factor in the guise of the Fremantle Doctor – a hot wind that blows along the Perth coast during the Australian summer. And sailing in a 20- to 30-knot breeze becomes a habit.

ABOVE: *John Bertrand's 1983 Newport residence commemorated by a plaque (below).* LEFT: *a Perth car number plate with an America's Cup symbol (above); an advertisement outside a fashionable bar in Fremantle (middle); a slogan at the entrance to the Canadian syndicate's private zone (below).*

BELOW AND OPPOSITE: *buildings in Perth and Fremantle.*

Newport becomes a memory. For the Gilded Age of the J-Class, the America's Cup and Newport seemed made for each other. In Newport, the New York Yacht Club held sway – but here no more. Which had created more hullabaloo in Newport, the Australian victory or the American defeat? It is difficult to say. Both, in fact, were unexpected until the very last lap of the seventh race. Despite everything, Newport and Fremantle have some things in common. Both were colonies; both were developed as maritime centres and as military or merchant ports; and yachting provided each port with a vital impulse. But their traditions are different. If Newport can remain rich and happy as the East Coast capital of yachting without the Cup, then Fremantle has quickly got to adapt to a future it was completely unprepared for, and a future which is uncertain at best. Fremantle lacks the tens of millions of potential tourists that Newport has, those tourists who flock to see the residences on Bellevue Avenue and the restored Colonial American houses so skilfully looked after by the Newport Historical Society.

Western Australia boasts a population of two million inhabitants and tourists coming here will come from very far away. For the city of Perth, the America's Cup provides a tremendous opportunity for self promoting. In our trip towards the unknown, one thing remains absolutely certain: Perth will make the whole business as profitable as possible. Western Australia is preparing for a kind of Olympic Games, and as we all know, they only return to the same city after a long time.

With the transfer of the America's Cup to Australia, the whole event is suddenly modernizing itself, and sponsors and investors are assuming roles whose importance would have been unthinkable in the past. The new war is being run on different lines, and all those taking part are being asked to make a different kind of effort. Nothing will be exactly as it was in the past: this first-ever Cup in the southern hemisphere will attract a worldwide audience. The Australian victory sees an old game being played with completely new rules. The Cup will no longer be a sport, it will be a show, and it will also be an important source for developing the host town. Half a million tourists are expected to come to Perth between September '86 and February '87, and according to the forecasts being made by the Western Australian Tourism Commission, each tourist will spend a minimum of one thousand Australian dollars. And because they are thinking of tourist investment as well, the New Zealanders have even set up their own challenge.

Arcade

BELOW: *members of the New York Yacht Club Race Committee.*
RIGHT: *Newport Shipyard, base for the challenging and defending yachts and building site of numerous American 12-Metres.*

The one true element that continues where the past left off is man himself. So much has been said about technology and research, but more than ever before the America's Cup is a war between human brains and not electronic ones: it is a psychological war.

How many sleepless nights must the researchers have spent waiting for the results of their tests? How many men have woken up in the night with an idea for a great new keel running through their heads? 'The day after this America's Cup finishes is a black mystery. I'll cross that bridge when I come to it; right now I don't have time to think about the future.' These are the words of John Kolius, one of the American skippers. Even if we sit down to examine the investment plans, and even when we realize that the total budget of the challengers amounts to US $120,000,000 we must not stop thinking of the Cup as being a myth. The old magic may have

NEWPORT
OFFSHORE
Ltd.

LEFT: *the Trophy Room at the New York Yacht Club.* BELOW: *the America's Cup when still on the NYYC premises.* OVERLEAF: *an aerial view of the race course of the next America's Cup. In the background, Rottnest Island, a fashionable seaside resort frequented by the residents of Perth.*

gone, but the Cup is moving with the times.

The Cup continues to shine in the uppermost room of the Royal Perth Yacht Club. It sits on a new marble plinth, and it sits in all tranquillity. The fact is that it is its journey – and our journey – that has just begun. The all-conquering hero of all times has been vanquished, even though he may not always have been the better man. A new era is beginning, and so is the suspense. Whither lies the Cup's next resting-place?

The Challengers

At the start of a trial run in the February 1986 world championship. For the first time in the history of 12-Metres, the final result of a regatta was determined by a fleet race and not a match race.

America Without the Cup

The old Victorian ewer is called America's Cup, but it belonged in the fullest sense of the word to the New York Yacht Club. For over a century the Cup Match had been an entertainment for the Club's members, run largely at its whim. The night that the America's Cup was removed from the New York Yacht Club, it was ceremoniously carried through the chambers so that members could take one last look. Tears flowed, toasts were made, and hundreds of hands were allowed to touch the holy grail on the eve of its trip to Western Australia. At the same time, in a far larger sense, the Cup was put within the reach of sailors all over the United States. Freed from the New York Yacht Club, it was up for grabs in Fremantle.

The America's Cup was an icon of the sport, and, as its keeper, the New York Yacht Club, could claim to be the leader in American yachting. When the Cup left New York, its existing order and tradition were swept away, and along with them went many of the notions about America's yachting establishment. Suddenly everyone from used car salesmen to regional boosters and real estate hustlers had as much business pursuing the Cup as any New York financier. Losing the Cup was as invigorating to US yachting as winning was to Australian nationalism. After the seventh race of 1983, the New York Yacht Club ceased to be wed to the Cup, and all over America sailors started thinking about how to get it for themselves. For the first time in its history, the America's Cup became a truly national event. The old order was overturned, the establishment declared obsolete, and all the rules changed. It was a brave new world for 12-Metre racing, and no matter what happened, it would never be the same again.

Ten American syndicates had filed challenges with the Royal Perth Yacht Club by the deadline for the 1987 Cup Match. One of them was the New York Yacht Club, now shorn of all its special status. Some entries were from clubs that had associations with past Cup skippers or past defence aspirants. Some of the challengers were serious, some not, and some were money making schemes, pure and simple. No matter what the connection or motivation, each of the challenges quickly found that in the brave new world of American 12-Metres competition dreams of instant success quickly turn into the reality of hard work.

No country in the world has built and campaigned as many 12-Metre yachts as the United States, but the actual number of designers, skippers, builders, and managers with experience in the Cup is surprisingly small. In the case of designers, all but one of America's successful '12s' were designed by the New York firm of Sparkman & Stephens. Others had tried, and several Sparkman & Stephens alumni are active in the field, but only the brilliantly sailed *Weatherly* of 1962 had bettered the Sparkman & Stephens boats, and successfully defended the Cup.

The builders of 12-Metres in the United States are centred between New York and Cape Cod, and most of the experienced organizers of the previous campaigns are similarly grouped. The skippers, tacticians, and sailmakers for the boats are scattered all around the country, however, and they were quickly sought out by prospective challengers. For a club to have a prayer of success in attracting financial support for the 1987 challenge, it needed some talent from previous campaigns, and the proven racing skippers provided the most visible and available talent around. Without a skipper, a challenge had no hope at all.

A credible 12-Metre skipper made fund raising at least possible, but without one the challenge was doomed. The Spider Lane Yacht Club challenge faded after raising virtually no money, and the Blue Dolphin Yacht Club, which was created for the purpose of mounting a challenge and making a lot of money, followed suit. Neither the Sag Harbor Yacht Club of New York nor the St Petersburg Yacht Club, of Florida, could inspire backers to part with cash. Having a skipper, and even a designer and builder on hand does not guarantee success, because success in mounting a 12-Metre campaign depends on money, and money raising in the United States was entirely changed when the Cup left for Australia.

The America's Cup was once the province of the mightily wealthy, men who could build, campaign, and then scrap giant yachts using only their pocket money. As times changed the yachts became smaller, yet relatively more expensive, so syndicates of millionaires were required to finance them. Then the *Intrepid* campaign of 1974 used a tax court ruling to declare their boat as part of an educational institution and the money spent on her campaign became tax-deductible. Funding suddenly became easier, since many people would rather give their dollars to sail boat racers than to the Government.

Educational 12-Metres are still the rule, but after 1983 the cost of campaigning a 12-Metre went through the ceiling. In the recent past $US 3,000,000 was considered a healthy amount for a domestic cup defence. For the 1987 challenge, some teams are budgeting over $US 16,000,000. To raise that kind of money you have to go beyond the local millionaire enthusiasts, so for the first time in history, American sailors began to seek actively corporate sponsorship. The search for corporate dollars quickly led all the players to the financial centre of America, New York. Unfortunately, for the others, there was already a yacht club in New York.

The New York Yacht Club took first helpings from the corporate community, in the form of a $1,000,000 donation from the Cadillac division of General Motors, and had first choice in the talent pool as well. In addition, the membership of the club included people with powerful ties in the media and advertising, and the New Yorkers cornered the services of their 'in house' designers, Sparkman & Stephens. In the face of this power, only one other East Coast challenge survived to 1986.

Three thousand miles west of Wall Street, California has a near monopoly on the remaining Cup asset, skippers. On the West Coast three challenges made the transition from talking to sailing, in large part because of the pool of sailing talent there. Overseas the America's Cup syndicates may bank on their famous financial or social connections, but in California, the personalities and careers of the skippers form the advertising message.

Six American syndicates accumulated enough expertise and money to survive until 1986. Each then signed contracts to build new boats for the 1987 Cup. Taken together, their efforts exemplify the way that America has responded to all kinds of major challenges, from World War II to the space race. After the shock of loss in Newport, the Americans mobilized all the design and sailing talent available, and are setting out to bury the opposition beneath an avalanche of preparation. Since the Cup went down under, three existing American '12s' have been significantly modified in order to match the performance *Australia II* displayed in Newport. These three became trial horses for the ten new boats on the drawing boards, all scheduled for completion in time to ship to Western Australia. Each new boat costs half a million dollars to build and equip, excluding the millions spent on design and testing. Within this massive outpouring of time and money, the individual syndicates maintain unique personalities and styles. The skills and resources, strengths and weaknesses of the six surviving American challenges are easy to pick out, but it is almost impossible to choose a true favorite for the long battle to recapture the America's Cup.

SAN DIEGO YACHT CLUB "SAIL AMERICA"

Dennis Conner, the skipper of the *Stars and Stripes* stable of 12-Metres, is an enigma to most sailors. Conner has few of the attributes traditionally associated with winning yachtsmen. He seldom appears to be having fun. He is not notably successful in business or some other field, and he does not spring from a sailing family. He is not a smooth salesman, nor can he tell a joke well. He is ill at ease in large social gatherings, and the tales of his social gaffes in boardrooms and cocktail parties are almost legend. Dennis is an easy mark for flatterers and sycophants, and since 1983 he has had uncertain faith in his abilities to handle all the concerns of a 12-Metre effort. But Conner brings one great asset to an America's Cup challenge, and that is that he may be the best 12-Metre sailor in the world.

If professionalism can be defined as the eradication of mistakes, then Conner is a blatant professional. Until Conner, most sailors played at the game, while he was working at it. In fact, he is driven by sailing. His results have been spectacular, and his book *No Excuse to Lose* is a bible of yachting. In that book Conner outlined the steps he takes when preparing for a major regatta. He laid out his methodical step-by-step approach. Many sailors were sure Conner would get a rude awakening when he attempted to use that method in the 12-Metre arena, where time and money considerations are paramount. To their surprise, Dennis intensified his style for the America's Cup, and the result was the 1980 route and victory over Australia.

Conner made it plain that if anyone wanted to beat him, they would have to play his game. His contemporaries complained, kicked, screamed, and finally followed his lead. Even Tom Blackaller, who despises this kind of sailing, had to endure a Conner-type campaign in 1983. Conner shrugged off the criticism and complaints by pointing out that every serious olympic sailor has to train that way, and he was certainly as intent on winning as any olympic contender. With his obsession for victory, it is a wonder that Dennis Conner survived losing the America's Cup. In a way, he did not, because like many of his team mates in 1983, he does not really believe the Cup was lost. He thinks it was stolen.

Conner's Sail America effort is imbued with the spirit of unfinished business. Key members of the '83 team still snarl when they talk about the way the New York Yacht Club ignored and then mishandled the questions concerning the legality of *Australia II*. They tell stories of spying, electronic surveillance, of lying and blackmail. In their eyes, Alan Bond is the Gadaffi of international sport. Like the Samurai of some Japanese epic, they have nursed their anger and grief, and sworn oaths of vengeance. They are confident in their cause, and in the face of all obstacles are sure they will return with the Cup. They have also put the lessons of '83 to work.

One failure in '83 was Conner's attempt to oversee the entire program. So for '87 he chose a different path. If '12s' had become high-technology, then they would use the aerospace industry for a model of organization. Sail America formed a design team consisting of Britt Chance, Bruce Nelson, and Dave Pedrick, plus a host of specialists, then gave the job of overseeing their work to John Marshall, of Hinkley Yachts.

Removing Conner from the design process was one of the first steps towards solving some of the problems of 1983. Free of the design responsibility, he could concentrate on organizing a sailing program, and touring the country looking for money. Business management of the team was largely out of his hands, and he finally devolved to the role that suited him best, running the sailing program in Honolulu.

Hawaii was perfect for Dennis' kind of program. No crowds, few prying eyes, and lots of wind and

Syndicate President	MALIN BURNHAM
Designers	BRITTON CHANCE BRUCE NELSON DAVID PEDRICK
Skipper/Helmsman	DENNIS CONNER
Names of boats	STARS & STRIPES 1, 2, 3
Names of trial horses	LIBERTY, SPIRIT OF AMERICA

sunshine. On the lumpy waters of the Molokai Channel, Conner and his team raced the '83 loser, *Liberty*, against a completely redesigned *Spirit*, renamed *Stars and Stripes*. A new *Stars and Stripes* followed in 1985, and she proved immediately superior to the rebuilt boat, which in turn was better than *Liberty*. In early 1986, yet another *Stars and Stripes* was christened in Hawaii, this one more radical than the last, and before the paint was dry on this boat, the team announced that one more would be built before they went to Australia. Conner's competitors called all of this 'full scale tank testing'.

Full scale tank testing does not come cheap, and Conner's budget has been estimated at over $16,000,000. This includes months of computer modelling and program writing, tank testing, construction of four 12-Metres (including the total rebuild of the old *Spirit*), nine months of daily sailing in Honolulu, over $US1,000,000 for sails, and of course all the logistical paraphenalia required to support the team in Fremantle for seven months. Sail America is firmly entrenched in second place in the funding race (behind the New York Yacht Club) but the budget is so large that a very major contribution in early 1986 was devoted solely to paying the interest on the loans that the team had taken out to finance the campaign.

Despite continuing money problems, which are the common denominator of all the American syndicates, the Sail America program has been almost perfect for Conner. He does not have the kind of veto power he held in 1980 and '83, but he has the freedom to run the sailing effort exactly as he wishes. So he has done everything possible to be the fastest person in Perth. The nature of the design effort was a classic example of this kind of Conner system.

Dennis believes that he can optimize any boat he is given. His big worry is that someone else will have a faster basic boat, hence the huge variations in the designs of the three *Stars and Stripes*. Each one was built to lines that had showed maximum promise in the team's complex computer performance prediction programs. The first new boat, *Stars and Stripes '85*, was fast right out of the box, and it may be the favorite of the camp. The second boat is quite different, with deep chine that extends beneath the waterline forward, a radical keel, and more sail area than the first boat. The third boat, one that Conner did not even want (he would rather spend another $US500,000 on sails) is a refinement of the two earlier ones, but again a design that the computers say will be faster. It will spread its sails in the 30-knot tradewinds of Honolulu just before the team leaves for Australia.

Conner is at his best when he is sure that no one else has worked harder or longer to perfect his boat and crew. With that knowledge safely in hand, he is free to concentrate on the business of sailing, and sailing is what he does best. Prior to the 1980 Cup challenge, Conner sailed for hundreds of days, summer and winter, becoming familiar with every nuance of 12-Metre driving. Working with John Marshall, then president of North Sails, and Tom Whidden of Sobstad, the team created the best 12-Metre sails yet seen. In 1983, Conner concentrated on tactics, believing that 12-Metre design had stagnated, and that tactics would win the Cup. He paid dearly for that mistake. For 1987, he has tested a flotilla of boats, and trained for over a year. The confidence that is engendered by this kind of program is written all over the Sail America camp Dennis put it succinctly one day as he crashed his boat through a Molokai whitecap. 'Look at these boats, look at this crew. Pretty Good, Huh? Do you really think anyone is going to be better than these guys? Who do think is going to beat us?' For Dennis the answer is 'no one'.

ABOVE: Stars and Stripes, *the Sail America syndicate yacht which was launched with the San Diego Yacht Club colours.* BELOW: *right, Dennis Conner, defeated skipper in 1983, preparing for the approaching vendetta on training waters off Hawaii.*

ABOVE: Stars and Stripes *'83 and* Stars and Stripes *'85 in a training session.* OPPOSITE: *an aerial view of the ex-*Spirit, *rejected contender for the defence in 1983 and subsequently re-christened* Stars and Stripes *'83, somewhat modified and adorned with the colours of Dennis Conner's new syndicate.* OVERLEAF: *the two San Diego challengers, crossing.*

12
12
US-40
US-40

USA

NEW YORK YACHT CLUB "AMERICA II SYNDICATE"

Honor dictated that the New Yorkers be first to challenge for the Cup. The New York Yacht Club had lost it, and it was their job to get it back. The Club had no experience at challenging for a Cup they had so long defended, so they fell back on some old familiar forms. A rump version of their old selection committee was set to the task of naming a syndicate to run their challenge. Three Cup organizations auditioned for the right to fly the Club's banner. One was led by Dennis Conner, one supported John Kolius, the American runner-up during the previous summer, and one was directed by Leonard Green, the wealthy inventor who owned *Courageous*.

The field dwindled as it became apparent that the transplanted Texan, John Kolius, had an inside track for the job. Conner, the Club's skipper for the last two Cup defences, announced that he was forming his own campaign and withdrew from the contest. He wanted to fire the New York Yacht Club before the Club could fire him. Soon thereafter, the New York Yacht Club placed its standard in the hands of Kolius and the team that supported him.

John Kolius is an excellent sailor. He won the Soling silver medal at the 1976 Olympics, and he was world J-24 champion. At his side for the 1983 and 1987 campaigns was the American John Bertrand, a Laser and Finn champion who won the silver medal at the Los Angeles games in 1984. Kolius' team had obvious on-the-water skills, and some experience in managing a complex 12-Metre campaign, but most important of all, it brought along the elixir needed to inspire a cup challenge – money. As the nabobs of the New York Yacht Club would soon discover, that money came with terms the Club had never before encountered.

The New York Yacht Club had long been the conduit for outside talent and funds, and one of the earliest sources of these funds was the state of Texas. Over the years the Texans developed their own version of the Cup tradition, combining sophistication and a 'Good ole Boy' Western outlook. They were tempted to mount their own campaign for 1987, but decided that it would be easier to work with the New York Yacht Club one more time. The unspoken truth of that arrangement was that it would be much easier to work with the Club, if it selected a Texan to be skipper. As soon as Kolius came on board, the Club received a multi-million dollar loan from OL Pitts, and the campaign was on its way.

OL (Oliver Lee) Pitts and his side-kick Lee Smith are institutions around the Cup scene. As ambassadors for the Fort Worth Boat Club, and representatives for a larger group of Texans and Oklahoma enthusiasts, they mix real power with an almost child-like capriciousness. Pitts is a diminutive gnome in his seventies, who looks more like a broad-bellied fairy tale shoemaker than a hard-thinking entrepreneur. Smith resembles a tall Texan classic cowboy, gone a bit soft around the edges. Together they make a Mutt and Jeff team that could anchor a TV situation comedy. They enjoy being just a couple of the guys, and they do take their fun seriously. After enjoying a few seasons in Newport, the pair decided that it was too difficult to secure a table for a really good meal. Their solution was to buy the oldest licensed establishment in America, the White Horse Tavern, established 1673, and make it the best restaurant in town.

In Fremantle they took a similar tack. They made lodging simpler by buying up apartment buildings, and in the process of establishing themselves, the pair became unofficial ambassadors for the New York Yacht Club. In Australia, that job is about as easy as being the PLO envoy to Tel Aviv, but the two Texans almost succeeded in winning over the locals. Their style is much closer to the Western Australian's rough and tumble way of doing things than it is to the studied coldness of the 'infamous' New York Yacht Club. When the team needs an unofficial spokesman to soften the blow of some

Executive Director	THOMAS F. EHMAN, JR.
Designer	M. WILLIAM LANGAN
Skipper	JOHN W. KOLIUS
Names of boats	AMERICA II US-42, US-44, US-46

official act, Lee or OL will get the nod. So far this campaign has had a lot of blows that needed softening.

The New York Yacht Club is nothing if not political, and the behind the scenes infighting began the moment the team was selected. In the past the syndicates were closely chaperoned by the Club. For the 1987 challenge, that order is somewhat reversed. This time outside operators, be they corporate sponsors, like Cadillac, or Texan benefactors, like OL Pitts, control the purse strings, and political power lies in courting those operators rather than the old guard at the New York Yacht Club. The *America II* syndicate also represents 32 other yacht clubs in an attempt to garner national support, so the rules have been changed drastically within the New York Yacht Club and the hierarchy is unclear. The result has been an ongoing confusion over where the power resides.

America II's management problems have been displayed in many ways over the last two years. One of the worst fiascos occurred in late 1985, when John Kolius announced his retirement from the *America II* group, citing political problems within the syndicate. In the past winners, world champions, and popular heroes had all been dismissed with imperious disregard for personal feelings or loyalties. This time, however, a grim little OL Pitts went to work twisting 'his boy's' arm, and flexing his own muscle with the New York Yacht Club. Within days, Kolius was back at the helm. It was very hard to say no to the man who holds the mortgage on the campaign.

John Kolius almost attracts controversy. More in the mold of Ted Turner than any other Cup sailor, Kolius is a favorite of the press, of the crews that sail with him, and of the groupies who follow the 12-Metre camps from port to port. All of this upsets many old-time club stalwarts, men who never liked Turner and consider Kolius uncouth and overrated. Kolius is goodlooking, straight-talking, and deceptively skilled at the psychological battles that are a part of any major sailing event. He also shows little patience for people in positions of authority who have less knowledge or skill than he does. This is almost a perfect recipe for conflict in a group that still carries the memories of decades of absolute New York Yacht Club control.

Happily for Kolius and the rest of the team, the New York Yacht Club has spent most of its time politely making life difficult for the other challengers. *America II*, US 42, was the first new American boat in the water after the loss of the Cup. There were many people who questioned the wisdom of building so quickly, but none could fault the fund raising sense of having a 12-Metre training in Australia two years before the match. Since she had no trial horse, the early work with the boat was mainly conceptual: testing various keel, rudder, and rig configurations. She also served as a tremendous tool for the people tracking down sponsorship. The other teams were still talking about boats, while the New Yorkers were sailing their boat, and sailing it in Australia.

The second boat explored design parameters that were out of reach for US 42, no matter how many appendages they stuck on her. The third boat, US 46, is intended to combine the best features of the first two into a medium-length, light-displacement 12-Metre that will serve the Club well from the light winds of the October races all the way to heavy going of February. Boat design apart, the biggest question hanging over the New York Yacht Club syndicate is whether or not the politicians and power seekers in the organization will allow their skipper and crew to get on with winning the Cup. They could easily drive their helmsmen mad before he has a chance to drive *America II* to victory, but if the team starts well, and shows consistent speed, Kolius should have a clear course in Australia.

B2
N04 B-2
USA

LEFT: America II, *US 42 and* America III, *US 44, the two New York Yacht Club contenders, crossing.* ABOVE: *John Kolius, skipper for the NYYC and ex-Soling champion.*

ABOVE: America II *and* America III *training off Fremantle.*
BELOW, left: *Olin Stephens;* right: *John Bertrand, second helmsman and tactician of* America II. OVERLEAF: America II *in the world championship held in February 1986.*

USA
USA

AMERICA II

US 42
H

NEWPORT HARBOUR YACHT CLUB "EAGLE SYNDICATE"

A review of the *Eagle* challenge roster makes it clear how California sustains three separate Cup challenges. *Eagle*, the third, and perhaps most tenuous of the Californian teams, has a pedigree and roll call that reads like a who's who of match racing.

In the position of chief advisor sits Bill Ficker, a past Star Class world champion, and winner of the annual Congressional Cup in Long Beach, an event that brings the world's best match racers to California. This personable, shiney-pated architect skippered *Intrepid* in 1970, and beat a faster Australian boat to keep the Cup safe in New York. Despite this triumph, Ficker never served upon the New York Yacht Club Cup Committee. Jerry Driscoll, a San Diego boat builder, is director of operations for the syndicate. Jerry is another Congressional Cup winner, and his crew amassed the best record in the 1974 Cup trials aboard *Intrepid*. That year the New York Yacht Club chose *Courageous* to defend. Both of these men have their reasons to hope that the America's Cup never re-enters the stuffy salons of the New York Yacht Club. In the positions of skipper and designer, the team has two men who have more than served their apprenticeships in the Cup business. One is a true all-American boy, the other is a citizen of the world.

John Valentijn, the designer of *Eagle*, is a one-man international cartel. Dutch by birth, Valentijn worked for Sparkman & Stephens, then travelled around the world to design America's Cup contenders for Australia, France, and the United States. Unfortunately for John, he was the designer of *Liberty*, the boat that lost the America's Cup.

Valentijn has always been willing to try something different in his boats. *Australia*, designed for the 1977 challenge, was the first contender to be smaller than her contemporaries, and she was followed by two more 'small' '12s'. The first was *France III*, with a keel that was articulated in order to operate as an airplane wings does, with a wide range of hydrodynamic shape. That idea died at the hands of a sixty-year-old skipper who was not up to solving its problems or exploiting its potential. *Magic*, designed for Dennis Conner's 1983 program, was intended to demonstrate that a small boat with a large sail area could excel, and she was half-right. What she lacked was a keel like the one Lexcen put on *Australia II*, one that would let a light 12-Metre behave like a heavy one. Through all of these trials, and they have been trials, Valentijn has remained a classic Dutchman: taciturn, a bit grumpy, with a cutting wit, and a philosophical acceptance of the mistakes one can make designing '12s'. 'How will you know if you don't try?'

'Designing a 12-Metre used to be 90 per cent art and 10 per cent science,' he says, 'now it is 75 per cent science and 25 per cent art.' The scientific search for *Eagle*'s design has taken Valentijn and his small band of contract computer specialists, aerodynamicists, and hydraulic engineers into uncharted regions. While out there, they came upon a design concept that Valentijn calls 'not quite revolutionary'. According to John, the faltering progress of the group's early fund raising may have worked in their behalf, since it kept them from building a boat during the first rush to get in the water. Back when *America II* was already sailing in Fremantle, *Eagle* was no more than computer codes around the country. Unable to build, the team explored the more radical features of the design, and were able to incorporate them into the boat, without having a compromise forced upon them by a building schedule.

The novice race watcher may not be able to pick out the nuances that make one boat radical and another old-fashioned, but that novice will have no

Project Manager	BILL CRISPIN
Designer	JOHN VALENTIJN
Skipper	ROD DAVIS
Name of boat	EAGLE
Name of trial horse	MAGIC

problem spotting Valentijn's *Eagle*. She sports a flamboyant paint scheme unheard of in America's Cup history. A 30-foot lone screaming eagle is emblazoned along the yacht's topsides. His claws stretch forward, reaching, according to the syndicate members, for the nearest kangaroo. In a field of yachts that includes mascot birds as varied as kiwis, kookaburras, and piping shrikes, the eagle of *Eagle* is in a class by itself. Valentijn is, of course, hoping that the long delayed yacht will also be in such a position.

The problem with postponing boat construction is that a team has less time to test the product once it is in the water. Revolutionary or not, it takes time for a crew to learn a boat's idiosyncrasies, and it takes hundreds of hours of practice for a skipper and crew to extract the best performance from the yacht. Happily for Valentijn, he is teamed up with a skipper who has been preparing for this Cup challenge for nearly a decade.

Rod Davis seems almost painfully old-fashioned at times. He is uncomfortable in the role of sailing rock star. He does not go out of his way to gossip with reporters, nor does he spend time making up rumours about his competition. He rarely discusses his own skills, and his emotions play on his face like the weather on a bare hillside. Anger clouds it, and success makes it beam; his gestures seem to come from a theatre director of another era, and only his obsession with the coming Cup series can detract from his uncommon politeness. Davis is proof that nice guys can finish first.

Davis' first America's Cup experience was aboard *Enterprise*, a boat skippered by Lowell North in 1977. Rod was the bowman that year, responsible for everything that happened up on the very tip of the vessel. In the decade since the *Enterprise* campaign began, he has made the pilgrimage all the way back to the helmsman station, and he has done it in style. Davis has won championships in numerous classes, under numerous flags. As an employee of North Sails, he has skippered boats for customers around the world, and taken many of them into the winner's circle.

Despite his success as a skipper, Davis is not above crewing with others. He was crew on board the Soling world champion in 1979, the national champion in 1980, was the pointman on the 1984 gold medal winner at the olympics. During the period when the owners of 80-foot, million-dollar yachts were flying him around the world to sail with them, Davis was happy to be part of someone else's olympic program. He has that kind of dedication to the sport.

Rod's America's Cup preparation includes most impressive victories at the Congressional Cup. He finished second in 1980, and won in 1981 and 1985, in both cases beating other America's Cup hopefuls. He also won a similar match racing event in New Zealand, and another aboard 80-foot ocean racers off California. Add to that his role as tactician aboard the 1984 12-Metre world champion, and a stint as mainsheet trimmer aboard one of the 1983 contenders, and you have someone with plenty of match racing and 12-Metre experience.

A unique complication to Rod's *Eagle* effort, is the fact that his wife, Liz, is the sister of Tom Schnakenberg. Schnakenberg is another North employee, and the man responsible for the winning sails aboard *Australia II*. He is the exclusive sailmaker for Bond's defence of the Cup this time around. Davis maintains that family ties will not deter him in his quest for the Cup. In fact, very little will deter him. 'Just give me and the crew an equal boat, it doesn't have to be the fastest, and I think we can win it all.'

ABOVE: *Rod Davis at the wheel of* Eagle, *the Newport Beach syndicate 12-Metre yacht. In the background, the trial horse* Magic.
LEFT: Eagle.

ABOVE: Eagle, *sailing close to the wind off the Californian coast.* RIGHT: *John Valentijn and Rod Davis, respectively designer and skipper for the* Eagle *syndicate.* LEFT: *a close-up of* Eagle*'s prow with its aggressive bird emblem painted on the hull.* OVERLEAF: Eagle.

US

CHICAGO YACHT CLUB
"HEART OF AMERICA CHALLENGE"

Faith has been the watchword of the Chicago Yacht Club's challenge for the America's Cup. One needed faith in an organization that had never before shown interest in the Cup; faith in a design house that had never drawn a 12-Metre. One had to believe that an admiralty court would consider Lake Michigan an arm of the sea. It required great faith to presume that the America's Cup could excite midwesterners. Finally, it required faith in a skipper who had never set foot on a 12-Metre. Of all the unlikely components of the Chicago challenge, the skipper was by far the easiest to believe in.

Buddy Melges, the skipper of *Heart of America*, is almost a folk hero to freshwater sailors. Melges hails from the middle of the country, an area known more for cornfields and dairy farms than sailing boats. He is the undisputed admiral of a navy of small boat racers in the United States. He is so happy in his place that no one can remember him ever looking for a berth on the big ocean racers that are the usual haunts for sailors of his caliber.

Using the 'down-home' humor of Will Rogers and a folksy common sense approach to sailing, Melges has made Zenda, Wisconsin, a world-famous yachting venue. 'Zenda isn't the end of the world,' he likes to tell supporters, 'but you can see it from there'. One of his best friends and protégés at the end of the world was a young Australian who worked for the nearby North Sails loft. In fact, that sailmaker made it possible for Buddy Melges to seriously contemplate a trip to Fremantle. If John Bertrand had not won the seventh race in 1983, Melges would never have thought about sailing '12s'. They never seemed enough fun for Buddy.

Melges loves speed. That is one reason why he has avoided many of the 'standard' routes to racing fame. Instead of ocean racers, he perfected his technique in Lake scows, boats that are surpassed in speed only by catamarans and the special Lake Garda designs in Italy. In the winter, when the lakes freeze solid, Melges goes ice-boating, and nothing under sail can match an ice boat for sheer exhilaration.

On the occasions that Melges has stepped away from his farm-edged lakes and specialty racers, he has spread terror through the ranks of his coastal brethren. He raced Solings, for a few seasons. He won a couple of North American championships, and represented the United States in the olympic games. He brought the gold medal home from Germany. From Solings he went on to the Star class, usually considered the most competitive of all the international keelboats. Buddy won the world championships in San Francisco, home court of Tom Blackaller. He beat everyone, in every race and that did wonders for his sailmaking business.

As recently as 1983 Melges did not know how a winch worked on a boat. He never sailed boats big enough to need them, and he had no desire to do so. When asked to give some good advice to student sailors, he came up with a hint about watching for the backs of cows and the fronts of birds, since birds always face into the wind and cows away from it. 'Some of my best races, I owe to cows,' he said.

There is a refreshing candor about the Chicago effort. The team tactician, Gary Jobson, announced that if the boat was a dog in trials, then they would not bother going to Australia. Would the boat be a dog? 'It's the first one they've ever designed, I think there's a high probability of that.' In Victoria, Canada, Melges announced to the assembled press that the rebuilt Canadian racer, *Canada I*, was 'the fastest 12-Metre in the world', hardly talk to reassure the financial backers on Lake Michigan. In Fremantle, Buddy declared that the behavior of the New York Yacht Club syndicate, 'makes me sick'. Hardly a phrase to warm the hearts of his countrymen.

Syndicate Chairman	EUGENE M. KINNEY
Design team	GRAHAM & SCHLAGETER
Skipper	HARRY C. "BUDDY" MELGES, JR.
Name of boat	HEART OF AMERICA
Names of trial horses	CLIPPER, DEFENDER

The Chicago trial horse is *Clipper*, a boat they call 'the old blue stove', because it exhibits the sailing qualities of an iron woodburner. After they had an especially successful weekend of racing against the 'evolutionary' *USA* from the Golden Gate team, Buddy had the crew of the boat shroud the underbody. Why? 'So the world doesn't see how far back we set yacht design today.'

It is an article of faith in Chicago that given a competitive boat, Melges will be the challenger for the Cup. This is not based on his match racing record, or his big boat experience, simply on his reputation as a hard-headed sailor. Of all the American skippers, Melges is probably the toughest, mentally. He needed all his resilience last spring, when his tactician, Gary Jobson, informed him that he would not be with the program in Fremantle. Jobson defended the Cup with Ted Turner in 1977, then fell into two dismal campaigns. First he went back with Turner in 1980, only to be crushed by Dennis Conner. Then he and Tom Blackaller were struck down by both Conner and Kolius in 1983. He has been on the rise for the last year, however, and he and Melges were a formidable team in the cockpit in the practice races.

At the same time Jobson was doing broadcast work on the upcoming Cup match, and the idea of yet another campaign (his fourth) could not compete with the chance to be a television commentator for the first time.

Buddy's response to losing his tactician was typical Melges. He thought of all the people who had ever beaten him in the international classes, and then checked off the ones on that list who had match racing experience. It is a statement of the strength of this year's Cup teams that almost all of the names on his last list are already sailing for another syndicate. One notable exception was Bill Buchan, Star Class world champion and olympic gold medal winner, who served on *Intrepid* in '74. Buchan, however, was not eager to go to Australia. This left Buddy eyeing the other teams, seeing which ones would fail, or who would be cast off on the way to Fremantle.

Even if Melges gets the tactician of his dreams, the entire question could down to the boat. *Heart of America* was designed by the firm of Graham and Schlageter, most famous for small ocean racers, and almost entirely unfamiliar with the International Rule for metre boats. Melges likes to call their design effort 'high technology from down on the farm', but their boat has much in common with the work of the French 12-Metre *French Kiss*. Both boats feature a high bow (to ward off the steep West Australian waves), a relatively low freeboard aft (to cut down on the weight of the yacht's hull), and a broad stern that is more in keeping with ocean racing design. *Heart of America* has a more 'traditional' *Australia II* keel than the French boat.

The Heart of America syndicate has kept expenses low, partly from necessity, and has been fairly successful in raising money. Major donations came from telecommunications and computer firms, and the team worked to pay the bills as they came due. When *Heart of America* fitted out in Newport, Rhode Island, before tune-up racing with one of the *America IIs*, she was largely paid for. The fund-raisers said that there was money in the pipeline for all the sails and support that the team would need in Australia, so the afterguard did not have to spend time passing the hat for donations. That gives Melges and Jobson a 'why not win?' attitude.

Jobson, speaking as a television sportscaster, describes the Cup this way. 'If the boat sails as fast as she tests, Chicago will be there. If we're there, then all the guys in Fremantle will see how hard it really is to beat Buddy Melges.'

ABOVE: Clipper, *the Chicago Yacht Club's trial horse, in San Francisco Bay where she trained with* Canada I *and the new St Francis contender.* LEFT AND OPPOSITE: Heart of America*'s crew in one of her first test runs. She will participate in the selection trials for the Cup.*

ABOVE: *skipper Bud Melges (right) and Richard Stearns, sail coordinator.* LEFT: Heart of America*'s no 2 crew-member in action.* OPPOSITE: *the Chicago 12-Metre on Lake Michigan (note the high-tech sails designed by Sobstad).* OVERLEAF: *the* Heart of America *beats to windward.*

US·51
HEART OF AMERICA
U.S.A.

S.A.

ST FRANCIS YACHT CLUB
"GOLDEN GATE CHALLENGE"

The most potent cocktail of old and new in the America's Cup is being mixed in San Francisco, California. There the tradition of privileged yachting, a bohemian indifference to convention, and the realities of high technology are all whipped together like the frothy hangover cures produced at the bar of the St Francis Yacht Club.

The St Francis can lay serious claim to the title of finest yacht club in the United States. It represents one of the social peaks in a city where the display of wealth has been considered a civic duty since the California goldrush. The St Francis has a long history of club racing syndicates, so it was natural to expect it to leap to the forefront of a cup campaign. It was predictable that the rich men at the top would quickly form a cup team. It was expected. It did not happen.

The St Francis team began with a computer leasing executive who became so enthused at the idea of the America's Cup in San Francisco, that he sent in the challenge without mentioning it to the club. The computer leasor was joined by a dealer in luxury automobiles and a retired yacht equipment manufacturer to form the executive committee of the Golden Gate challenge. The Golden Gate challenge had the name of the yacht club on its stationary, but for many months there was little else attached to it. Like all the American challenges, it had to hunt down the money and the talent required to mount an effort. The money, even under the Golden Gate, was not easy to come by, but the bay area is rich in sailing talent.

Two men who personify the entire sailing community of San Francisco are heavily involved with the Golden Gate challenge. One is team's designer, Gary Mull and the other is the skipper/manager, Tom Blackaller. Both in their late 40s, they have worked with and against one another for decades. Throughout it all they have remained good friends, even though their only similarity is their overwhelming self-confidence.

Blackaller is tempestuous, brilliant, rude, inspiring, offensive, charming, insecure, and the possessor of an immense ego. A natural sailor and professional sailmaker, he races cars for relaxation. Blackaller has won in the most competitive of sailing classes, and his past performances put him on the same level as a Buddy Melges of the Chicago Yacht Club or a Dennis Conner. His style is entirely different, however. Blackaller has been called a 'an incendiary device' by his associates, and at full cry his braying laugh, his boasting, and his cackling critiques of the competition can be heard from one end of a marina to another. He has no patience at all for the plodding, self-disciplined Conner approach to racing and, the antipathy between these two Californians has almost become a vendetta.

Tom Blackaller does not like to test boats. He does not like to practice. He does not like restrictions. He does like to be in charge, and he has more experience at the helm of a '12', and in the long arduous business of campaigning one, than any one else in Northern California. So far he has harnessed that experience for the Golden Gate syndicate, and has proved to be a surprisingly capable administrator. The big question in San Francisco is whether Tom's ego will compel him to drive the yacht in Fremantle, or if he will share the helm with Paul Cayard, the number two helmsman in the camp.

The Golden Gate team enjoys similar talent in Gary Mull, the naval architect behind the effort. The breadth of his knowledge and the depth of his

Syndicate President	ROBERT D. SCOTT
Designer	GARY MULL
Skipper	TOM BLACKALLER
Helmsmen	PAUL CAYARD TOM BLACKALLER
Names of boats	USA 1, USA 2
Name of trial horse	DEFENDER

experience are remarkable, as he will happily point out. Mull is a very different kind of a San Francisco product, and he may be as much of a Renaissance man as any engineer could possibly be. This is due partly to personality, partly to happenstance.

The University of California at Berkeley, across the bay from San Francisco, is one of the most politically active, if not radical, schools in the United States, and one of the most strenuous engineering establishments. Mull is a product of both sides of the campus. His early training in literature has given him a rare appreciation for the ironies of his trade, while his wide experience working on projects from ships to sailboards has given him an understanding of his profession that very few yacht designers can match.

Mull, wearing his designer hat, will admit that either the last generation or the next generation of '12s' would provide more pleasant projects for a designer. 'Designing these boats, especially R–1, our revolutionary boat,' (the syndicate has two boats, one evolutionary and one far more radical) 'has been as interesting and challenging as any project could be. It hasn't been fun, but it has been challenging.' One of the reasons that the design has been less than fun, is that for the first time the 12-Metre community has been forced to consider all kinds of applied technology. 'It's like going back to school for eighteen hours a day.'

Gary is not alone in the design department. Sharing the spotlight is Heiner Meldnor, a fluid dynamicist from the Lawrence Radiation Laboratories, the establishment that thought up the 'star wars' space defence system, among other doomsday devices. Mull's other partner in the process is Alberto Alvares Caldron, an applied aerodynamicist who refuses to use the words port and starboard, or fore and aft. At times, the design team would argue fiercely over previous applications of computer codes or proof of some testing method, only to have one of the players suddenly declare that, 'I can't tell you that, it's classified'. Mull claims to have aged several years in the last 12 months, but he also maintains that the revolutionary Golden Gate 12-Metre will be so different that 'a person who has never seen a 12 will know that this is something special.'

Part of the trials and tribulations of designing the 'revolutionary' boat for the Golden Gate team, has been deciding which of the Darth Vader technologies to adapt to a sport as 12-Metre racing. 'We explored just about everything,' says Mull, 'including keels that were little more than saucers of lead hung from the hull by two or three foils.' Circular keels (so called 'napking rings'), split keels, perforated keels, and canard appendages were all part of the program. Just before going to press, Mull was able to confirm that the Golden Gate boat does not have anything like an *Australia II* keel. 'The hull of the new boat is very similar to our first one, but the appendages are like nothing you've ever seen on a boat.'

Mull, the observer of life, still finds time to laugh at the way the team and the yacht club have danced around one another. Other bay area clubs have put on extensive events on behalf of the '12', but, 'it took months before the St Francis members agreed to support the challenge'. He is sure they will be pleased with that support, however. 'Knowing what I know about this design, and knowing who will be sailing it, I will be very surprised if we don't win the America's Cup.'

ABOVE: USA, *the first 12-Metre designed by Gary Mull for the Golden Gate syndicate, sailing in San Francisco Bay toward Alcatraz Island which, if the syndicate manages to re-claim the Cup for America, will be the centre point of the triangular race course and, as such, a prime position for spectators.* BELOW: *right, the hull's interior; left, a close-up of her double helm.*

12
US-49
PACIFIC TELESIS

ABOVE: USA. BELOW: *Gary Mull, her designer.* RIGHT: USA *being towed under the Golden Gate on her way back from a training session. The man standing up is skipper Tom Blackaller.* OVERLEAF: *a close-up of her sails.*

PACIFIC TELESIS

YALE CORINTHIAN YACHT CLUB
"COURAGEOUS SYNDICATE"

ABOVE AND RIGHT: *two photos of* Courageous *in two of her evolutionary phases. In late spring 1986 the* Courageous *campaign had still not made the final decision on how it would pursue the challenge. Funds had long since dried up due to constant rebuilding and testing and no new sponsor had come to the fore. It was doubtful that she would actually compete.* BELOW: *the crew on parade.*

COURAGEOUS
IV
U.S.A.

ROYAL THAMES YACHT CLUB
"1987 BRITISH CHALLENGE FOR THE AMERICA'S CUP"

Yachting as a competitive sport was born in England, and the English, naturally enough, are among the main figures to be found in the history of the Cup. Had they not extended an invitation on the occasion of the Great Exhibition of 1851, the schooner *America* would never have been built. Not only that, the Hundred Guineas Cup would never have become the sporting, technical and traditional phenomenon that it is today.

For about a century, the Cup remained a kind of game for several personalities from British society, and for several groups of syndicates comprising important people on the American economic scene. Owning a yacht and taking part in the America's Cup was not merely a passion, but a status symbol as well. From James Ashbury, the first challenger, to Sir Thomas Lipton, and then to Peter de Savary competing for the Cup and standing up to the New York Yacht Club has always had connotations of social promotion. Of course, for anybody belonging to the Royal Thames Yacht Club or to the even more exclusive Royal Yacht Squadron, this was only of secondary importance.

In reality, though, the challenges made by the Royal Thames Yacht Club (founded in 1775) are few and far between. The first brought the schooner *Cambria* to New York in 1870. She was built by Ratsey at Cowes. The second challenge brought the 12-Metre *Sovereign* to Newport in 1964. Designed by David Boyd and skippered by Peter Scott, it came along with the *Kurrewa V*, used on the occasion as a trial horse. Although unable to bring off the challenge in 1974, the Royal Thames Yacht Club was named Challenger of Record, and it organized selection tests among the challengers.

In 1958, the Royal Yacht Squadron presented the 12-Metre *Sceptre*; in 1980, the Royal Southern Yacht Club launched the challenge that took *Lionheart* to Newport. And lastly, under the colours of the Royal Burnham Yacht Club, Peter de Savary presented *Victory* in 1983.

If English activity and creativity have played an important role in spreading the sport on an international scale, and if the creation of the RORC and of the Admiral's Cup have made offshore racing a sporting speciality of the highest level, then it should also be remembered that the first English presence at Newport in the era of 12-Metres was marked by a very definite inferiority. The victory of the defenders seemed a foregone conclusion, thanks to the help of Sparkman & Stephens and the superiority of the American skippers and sailmakers. From the technical and sports point of view, the level improved with *Lionheart*. In Howlett, England found a designer who was convinced of the value of research, and a designer who was already able to come up with some good, personal ideas.

The great figure of the 1983 challenge was Peter John de Savary, who launched a campaign on an unheard-of scale. First he bought *Australia* to use as a bench mark, and he had two boats built. The first was launched in 1982 and was designed by Ed Dubois; the second, the *Victory '83*, was designed by Ian Howlett. Many comments were made about his campaign methods, but in 1983 the English came close to success in coming second in the Louis Vuitton Cup, behind the Australians. Despite being motivated and generous, de Savary is not really the type one thinks of as belonging to the world of British yachting.

The new challenge is being made on a more discreet scale. Not surprising, considering that the 1987 British challenge for the America's Cup is being carried out under the banner of the Royal Thames Yacht Club, of which His Royal Highness The Prince of Wales is the Commodore. The approach this time is different, but in the key roles of this new group we come across many of the men who took part in the previous challenge.

Harold Cudmore is the race team manager and is, in practice, the skipper. He is an internationally-known helmsman, and winner of numerous com-

Syndicate Chairman	GRAHAM WALKER
Designers	IAN HOWLETT DAVID HOLLOM
Skipper	HAROLD CUDMORE
Names of boats	CRUSADER I, II ("HIPPO")

petitions of match racing (including the Lymington Cup six times over and the 1986 Congressional Cup). Cudmore also won the 1985 Admiral's Cup with *Phoenix*; he has also sailed on all the regatta courses in the world. He withdrew at Newport in 1982 'because he did not feel in sympathy with the way the programme was being run'.

Phil Crebbin will be the technical manager. Ian Howlett is heading one of the two research teams. Back in 1982, Howlett had already considered it important to explore the possibility of adopting wings on the keel; the Keel Boat Technical Committee of the IYRU confirms the legality of this insofar as the Universal Rule is concerned. By making this document public the English put themselves with the Australians over the keel gate controversy at the New York Yacht Club. David Hollom collaborated on the research, Acorn was the head of the project and is today the head of the second team. Hollom is a successful designer of remote-controlled models, and has worked in Laurent Giles's workshop. The first work phase of this English campaign was concluded without fuss. This was due principally to the decision to put the first of the funds collected into a massive research programme. Headed by Howlett, the group carried out an 'evolutionary' project – and thus was created the first *Crusader*. Andrew Claughton of the Wolfson Unit at the University of Southampton worked alongside Howlett. The various designs and tests with simulated wave motion were carried out with models on a 1:10 scale at the Wolfson Unit where, in 1980, Howlett had studied and perfected the bandy rig, which was immediately adopted by the Australians for the finals against *Freedom*.

In the next phase, carried out at the Royal Naval Establishment at Halsar, models on a 1:4 scale were used. Both the first and second boats were built in aluminium by Cougar Marine, on the Hamble, using the same expertise used to create *Victory '83*. Launched by the Princess of Wales, *Crusader* was first exhibited at the London Boat Show in 1986 and then sailed for the Fremantle base. The second boat arrived in Australia in May. While Howlett's 12-Metre was created as a relatively conservative reference point, the second project is decidedly more radical and, once more, the result stemmed from lengthy research. Hollom's team is made up of Stephen Wallace and Herbert Pearcy, a specialist in aerodynamic studies. Tests were carried out with simulated wave motion in the ship model basin for this second boat, with models on a scale of 1:10, at the Teddington Nautical Maritime Institute. The final stage of the tests was carried out at the National Maritime Institute Towing Tank at Feltham. Furthermore, a computer modelling programme was used for comparing the results given at the basin. British Aerospace helped with the research.

The 1987 British challenge for the America's Cup started off quietly enough, not because there was a lack of men or technological resources, but because a suitable financial structure had to be set up. From the outset, important companies such as British Airways and British Aerospace took an important part.

Strangely enough, sponsorship is uncommon. As marketing manager Nigel Hawkes puts it: 'This challenge is not linked to just one name. Nobody can say '*We* are the challenger' and use this for personal ends. This time we want to get through to the companies and to the public.' This financing plan is highly original. The British America's Cup Challenge Public Limited Company is a shareholder's company. Shareholders have the right to see the results of the research programmes, the right to use pictures, and are joint owners of the group's boats, bases and equipment. If victory comes their way, the shareholders will share in running the future defence and eventual profits. They also stand to lose in the event of an early elimination. The public is being asked to help conquer the America's Cup by means of the British Challenge Club: the annual subscription fee is £10.

LEFT: *a view of the deck of the 12-Metre* Crusader, *taken from its mast.* OPPOSITE: *above, Bruce Banks at the helm of* Crusader; *below, the British challenger sailing close to the wind.*

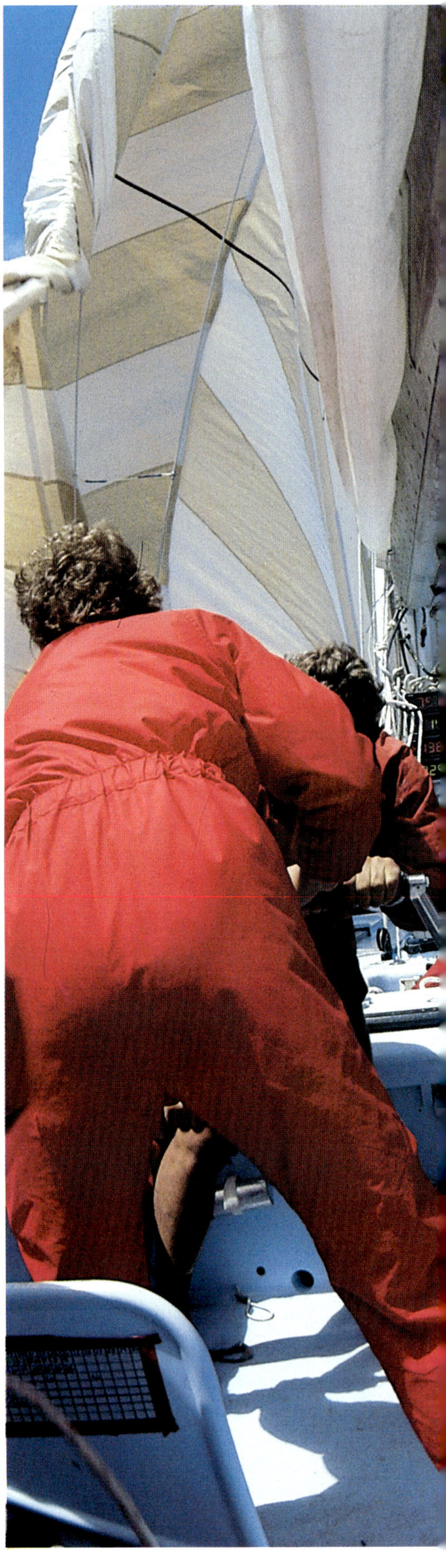

ABOVE: *Harold Cudmore, skipper for the British syndicate, in action.*
RIGHT: Crusader*'s crew getting to grips with the coffee-grinder while tacking.*

ABOVE: *the British yacht, designed by Ian Howlett, on a training session in the English Channel.* LEFT: *an aerial view of* Crusader. *After this picture was taken, the Royal Thames Yacht Club launched another 12-Metre designed by David Hollom.* OVERLEAF: *the British crew leaning over the windward side, sailing close to the wind.*

CRUSADER

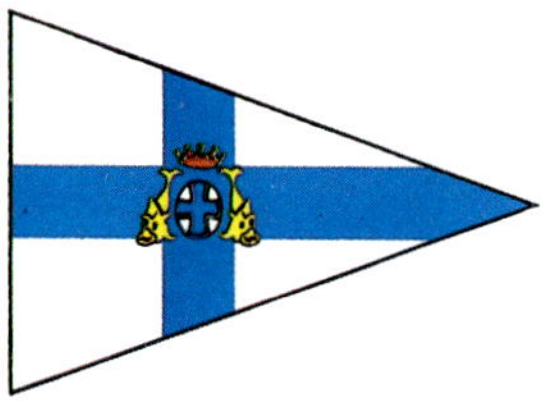

SOCIÉTÉ DES RÉGATES ROCHELAISES "CHALLENGE KIS FRANCE"

The America's Cup has become an affair of state in France. As they say there, it has 'gone democratic'.

The first person to arouse French interest in this unique event was Marcel Bich. He did so with a certain amount of flair, much in the spirit of the great yachtsmen who took part in the early days of the Cup, back in the nineteenth century.

The next to take part was Yves Rousset-Rouard, who received no State backing or indeed any funding at all when he participated in the Cup in 1983.

It was only in January 1984 that France realized that the America's Cup was an event that aroused worldwide attention, and that it would only be right for the country to take part in it.

The Socialist government which had done nothing to help Rousset-Rouard in 1983 now became a patron, pledging to do everything within its power to help not just one, but two, French challengers.

With the promise of official backing, the previous rather poor results obtained by French crews receded into the background, and wonderful forecasts for the future were made. Back in 1983, *France III* had made it as a challenger finalist before being ignominiously defeated – penniless, it is true, but without any debts.

So France, which had had such difficulty in scraping together $US1,000,000 for the Cup in 1983, made ready. State backing was to be to the tune of $US8–10,000,000 for the two challengers. The curtains were ready to lift on the French preparations.

Two years have gone by now, and things have come down to a much more mundane level (as they so often do in France), but the results are surprising all the same.

On the one hand there is Yves Pajot, the helmsman. The best man in France when it comes to sailing around three buoys, he is extremely capable, likeable, rather laid back and madly individualistic. He has charm, he is an optimist, he is a troublemaker, and he is incapable of getting a team together. Despite being a specialist at bringing off improvized strategies, he will never be a skipper in the America's Cup because he just cannot maintain his staying power over a long period.

Yves Pajot thus spent two years doing everything within his capabilities including training intensively from 1985 onwards with two crews, both in France and Australia, and with the best equipment available. The money for this first French challenge began to run out in 1986. The first sponsors had already supplied their share, but it looked as if the State was not going to cough up the funding it had promised. The new sponsors who were so vital to the project were in no hurry to provide funds either, very probably because they were nonplussed to see the media warfare that had been developed and perfected by Marc Pajot (brother of Yves) together with his professional sponsor, the Kis company. This first challenge was, therefore, in a very poor state indeed by the time the yacht, designed by Daniel Andrieu, was ready in Perth, and it is a great pity that Yves will not take part. And so this first and most public French challenge has sunk before the Cup has even started.

Several weeks before the Louis Vuitton Cup, the other challenger, headed by Marc Pajot, was ready. It is sponsored by the towns of La Rochelle and Sète, but especially by the Kis company. It is, in fact, a private retaliation against a public undertaking, and it has proved that the America's Cup is, was, and evermore shall be, an event for men alone – exceptional individuals who can make a decision and risk putting large sums of money into such a particular form of competition.

The Kis company is the only company in either the public or the private sector to have put so much money into the America's Cup – a total in the region of $US9,000,000. The yacht being sponsored with this enormous sum of money has been given the amusing name of *French Kiss*. Thanks to Philippe Briand's daring and talent in refraining from copying *Australia II* (which most of his fellow desig-

Syndicate Chairmen	Admiral MARQUEZE MARC PAJOT
Designer	PHILIPPE BRIAND
Skipper	MARC PAJOT
Name of boat	FRENCH KISS
Names of trial horses	FREEDOM, ENTREPRISE

ners have done) and coming up with a design that is both original and highly efficient in winds of over 15 knots, and thanks to Marc Pajot's professionalism, *French Kiss* has become one of the favourites for getting through the eliminating races of the Louis Vuitton Cup.

Kis was the first company to see the America's Cup as a huge boost to advertizing. The world's press has focussed in on *French Kiss*, whose name has kindled an affection amongst the public that a more serious name would never have succeeded in doing.

At which point you can stop and think for a moment. Either you will thank the stars that the America's Cup has become an advertizing stunt which will enable the competition to flourish, or you will deplore what is happening. At any rate, it would seem to be a necessary evil. Instead of fighting each other without any long-term hope of success, the international authorities should channel this trend towards advertizing in such a way as to curb the more harmful aspects. Neither *French Kiss*, *Azzurra*, the New Zealand boat, or any of the challengers have brought about 'advertising pollution', and that is the way it should stay; maintaining a delicate balance to preserve the traditions of the Cup by means of the all-too necessary sponsors, but without going overboard about the whole thing and letting the 12-Metres descend to the depths of the Formula I.

Before winning two races off Perth in February 1986, Marc Pajot had never been at the helm of a boat in an olympic race at international level before. His professionalism, his versatility and rigorous attitude, and the effect he has had on his crew have surprised more than just a few people. The fact is that Marc, like Dennis Conner, has all the necessary qualities for being a great skipper in the America's Cup – discipline, staying power, ambition, a little megalomania, a well-balanced character and a huge capacity for physical effort. Such are the qualities of Marc, even if he lacks his brother's charm (not much of a help in racing) and his instinctive talent.

For months Marc has been learning, taking notes, correcting and recording the techniques of match-racing. He has surrounded himself with good men, and has also succeeded in striking a good balance in his relations with his sponsor, Serge Crasnianski, a man with a personality as strong as his own.

Pajot and *French Kiss* are favourites for the Louis Vuitton Cup, but French technology is by no means a total stranger to this new undertaking.

The French are very good at sailing. Over the past five years they have carried off many Ton Cups and have come to the forefront of international multi-hull racing. Furthermore, a country which could dream up Concorde, the Mirage and the Excocet is also capable of doing a lot when it comes to technological research, and that is precisely what France has done. *French Kiss* is an out and out product of the computer age. It was neither thought up in a ship model basin nor even tested. The Dassault company (the people who build Mirage aircraft) put its engineers and computers to work on creating what is the most original 12-Metre since *Australia II*.

State backing has had good results where the sails are concerned. Up until now, the French were used to using composite fabrics imported from other countries as well as buying from sailmaking companies all over the world. The sails on *French Kiss* are 100 per cent French-produced, and the material is made in France as well. The sails are cut to size by small French sailmaking companies. The whole undertaking is French and as such is far more of a national effort than many of the yachts coming from other countries.

The only thing that remains to be seen is whether *French Kiss* can keep up the pace that she set herself at Fremantle in February, and whether Marc Pajot, for all his lack of experience, is able to use his sophisticated equipment to compete against the stars of match racing.

ABOVE: *angular view of* French Kiss*'s beautiful Australian base.*
RIGHT: *the French Philippe Briand design.*

LEFT: *an aerial view of* French Kiss. ABOVE: *skipper Marc Pajot.* RIGHT: *the Eiffel Tower illuminated by day for the celebration of the launching of the French 12-Metre held in Trocadero Square.* OVERLEAF: French Kiss.

FRENCH

SOCIÉTÉ NAUTIQUE DE MARSEILLE
"CHALLENGER FRANÇAIS POUR L'AMERICA'S CUP"

LEFT: *Yves Pajot, brother of Marc and helmsman of the would-be challenger* Challenge *(below). He will not be taking part in the 1986–87 America's Cup due to lack of funds, even though the Daniel Andrieu-designed yacht is ready.*

YACHT CLUB COSTA SMERALDA "CONSORZIO AZZURRA"

During the spring of 1895, a gigantic billboard in Italy showed the model of a boat inside a bottle: the 12-Metre *Azzurra*. The slogan chosen for the advertizing campaign of an insurance company read' 'We protect a dream'. It was quite true, for the *Azzurra* was never looked upon as being a mere boat by the Italians, but as something much more.

Today, the dream of long ago is no longer on its own – there are other 12-Metre craft competing to seize the national imagination and to represent the dreams of the Italians. The number of challengers rose to four in 1984 and four yachts left Italy for the Royal Perth Yacht Club. The fact is, that the myth of the success of *Azzurra* in 1983 has created a climate in which Italy has come to believe that it can win the Cup.

Right from the start, *Azzurra* had gone from the sports columns in the press into the front pages, something unthinkable for a yachting event. The victories of Straulino and Rode at the end of the 1950s were completely forgotten. It cannot be said that sailing is a popular sport in Italy in the 1980s, and in this case what turned the undertaking into a myth were not gold medals at all, but two well-known public figures who gave their weighty support to setting up and consolidating the first *Azzurra* consortium: Fiat magnate Giovanni Agnelli and HH Karim Aga Khan, the founder and president of the Costa Smeralda Yacht Club. Another person who contributed towards the credibility of the enterprise was Beppe Croce, president of the IYRU and an important figure for years at Newport, where he was president of the judges.

Back in the 1960s, both Agnelli and Croce had examined the possibility of organizing a first Italian challenge. An important element in the 1983 challenge (the same will hold true for the 1987 challenge) consisted of setting up the consortium as a pool of sponsors. Each of the companies sponsoring the challenge took part on an equal basis, and their aim was twofold: to promote the image of their products and generally to promote the image of things made in Italy. This idea had been successfully put into practice during the Swedish challenge of 1980.

Giovanni Agnelli and HH Karim Aga Khan gave their backing once again, and the challenge continued with the setting up of a new *Azzurra* consortium. Its president was Riccardo Bonadeo, a member of the executive committee on the previous undertaking. A realistic budget was established for the Australian challenge and backed up by 24 sponsors, each of which had an individual share of 600 million liras to pay.

In the meantime, the Costa Smeralda Yacht Club had purchased the 12-Metre *Freedom*. So as to boost its own international activities, it organized the 12-Metre class world championship at the end of the 1984 sporting season. Eight boats from five countries participated (those taking part were Australia, Canada, France, Italy and New Zealand). Much was expected of the competition between *Azzurra* and *Victory '83*, recently acquired by the newly set up *Italia* consortium. *Challenge 12* took part in the first stage of the championship as well; she had been purchased by the Viareggio group which had formalized a challenge under the colours of the Circolo Nautico Marina of Carrara. The man responsible for this initiative was Fabio Perini, who got Ben Lexcen and Tom Schnackenberg to come to Italy as consultants. Despite the fact that John Treharne and John Savage were aboard *Challenge 12* (both men came from Bond's group), the performance during the world championship was disappointing – some important sponsors backed out, and that particular operation was shelved once and for all. The fourth Italian group, from Portofino, had not been able to get past an initial promotional stage and had had to give up their option on *Spirit of America*.

When the world championship was held at Porto Cervo, it was announced that the Costa Smeralda Yacht Club would be a challenger at the first America's Cup to take place in the southern hemisphere.

Syndicate President	RICCARDO BONADEO
Designer	ANDREA VALLICELLI
Skipper	LORENZO BORTOLOTTI
Helmsman	MAURO PELASCHIER
Names of boats	AZZURRA 2, 3, 4
Name of trial horse	AZZURRA 83

Skippers of *Freedom* were Dennis Conner, then Tom Blackaller and lastly John Kolius, but the big news at the time was that *Azzurra* had lost against *Victory '83*. The public found this defeat difficult to swallow, and this was a first sign of the crisis that appeared 'after Newport'.

One year after that particular world championship, Mauro Pelaschier commented that 'the sporting aspect went off as it should have at Newport. Everything was going well: we had the money we needed, and some of the rival technicians were not up to our standards. I think that was when we began to pay more attention to our image than to the technical side of things. And yet when we returned home, Cino had said that we should be allowed to get on with our work and to make progress. But the truth is that we were unable to work seriously. By the time we got to the world championships at Porto Cervo, we were tired and demotivated . . .'

So what had changed since Newport? Cino Ricci had decided to switch from the well-deck to the role of technical adviser. Pelaschier and Nava remained on *Azzurra*, and Stefano Roberti was in charge of *Freedom*.

During the winter of 1984/5 the *Azzurra* men were among the first challengers to take part in a series of tests in the waters of Fremantle. *America*, US 42, took part as well: a programme of regattas and speed tests was carried out together with John Kolius's group. Following this, *Azzurra* worked together with the first *Kookaburra*. While all this was going on, the Vallicelli workshops were finishing off the project for *Azzurra '85*, following a series of tests in the model basin carried out at Wageningen. The naval division of the Industrie Meccaniche Scardellato of Treviso built the yacht, with Marco Cobau in charge. Once again the system introduced by the Vallicelli workshops – the longitudinal structure – was carried out on the second *Azzurra*.

The launching took place at the Naval Arsenal in Venice, at the end of July 1985. As far as time and schedules were concerned everything seemed to be going well but the problem concerning the crew was far from being solved. In point of fact, this crisis worsened when *Azzurra '85* had her first run-in with the old *Azzurra* in September of that year, at Porto Cervo.

Mauro Pelaschier fell out with the technicians and Stefano Roberti took over as first helmsman. Lorenso Bortolotti, who had looked after the sports organization of the Italia Consortium, went over to *Azzurra* as skipper. Between the discussions and the uncertainty about everybody's roles and responsibilities, the programme for completing *Azzurra '85* was delayed; already it had been held up by problems regarding roll (balance), and first the keel and then the mast were shifted in order to remedy this. At the end of the year the group set out for Australia once again. *Azzurra* started sailing at the beginning of January and so took part in the 12-Metre world championships. The news coming from these regattas showed that the situation had greatly deteriorated since Newport, and also since the world championships at Porto Cervo. The best result that Stefano Roberti and Lorenzo Bortolotti obtained was a fifth place. The great sky-blue dream of the Italians seemed to be crumbling more and more. Much of the blame was laid on the yacht and on the lack of attention paid to its proper completion. Before going back home to Italy, Ricci commented that 'even if it was a negative experience it was still an important one. The tests in the model basin showed that longer and heavier boats were needed for Fremantle than those that are studied for Newport. Here we were up against a wave factor more than against a wind factor. Medium or smaller yachts seemed to be more competitive in the conditions we experienced during the world championships – relatively lighter yachts, therefore – and so we're obliged to take another good-look at our ideas, but we're by no means the only ones who are going to do this.'

RIGHT: *Cino Ricci, skipper of* Azzurra *in 1983, now councillor general of Consorzio Azzurra.* ABOVE: Azzurra II. *It is very likely that either* Azzurra III *or* Azzurra IV *will run in the next America's Cup.* LEFT: Azzurra *training off the Sardinian coast.*

ABOVE: *Azzurra '83, the 12-Metre yacht that represented the first Italian challenge for the America's Cup at Newport.* BELOW: *Giovanni Agnelli at the wheel of the second vessel built for Yacht Club Costa Smeralda. At his side is the helmsman proper, Mauro Pelaschier.* OVERLEAF: *Azzurra '83.*

AZZURRA

YACHT CLUB ITALIANO
"CONSORZIO ITALIA"

Thanks to the effect that *Azzurra* had in 1983, the Italians discovered the America's Cup. Not only the Cup but also *Azzurra* herself had had such a resounding effect that there was a clamour for participation and for rivalry. Thus the *Italia* consortium was established under the colours of the Italian Yacht Club, the latter bringing class and tradition to the newcomer. Where experience was concerned, the two groups could have collaborated, but Italy is Italy and the America's Cup is the America's Cup, and collaboration is not always easy to come by as most of the competing countries have discovered.

The *Italia* consortium was set up by a small group of people in industry and finance, working with the Giorgetti & Magrini design workshops in Milan. Carlo Massimiliano Gritti, president of the Pilar Corporation, had a key role – he was the person who got the option on *Victory '83*. Two other equally important people are Maurizio Gucci and Gahil R Pharaon.

As far as communications are concerned, the group addresses itself to a public that is both informed and interested in yachting and the economy. This being so, the link with the Italian Yacht Club seems even more significant.

Founded in Genoa in 1879, the 'Royal' Italian Yacht Club has been linked to famous names and deeds for over a century, and is one of the most active sailing clubs in the Mediterranean. Its sporting activity started in 1897 with the creation of the Genoa International Regatta Week for formula classes. One year later, in 1898, the Duke of the Abruzzi offered the Coppa d'Italia as a trophy. In 1936, the 8-Metre *Italia* won the olympic gold at Kiel; four members of the Italian Yacht Club were aboard. The Giraglia regatta, a classic ocean race in the Mediterranean, was set up in 1952. There was no lack of ideas regarding a properly organized financial campaign, and right from the start, the competition between the two consortiums has been stimulating (despite all the discussions and arguments). The first clash came about over the name. The men of *Azzurra* feared that a 12-Metre yacht called *Italia* might well seem more of a national symbol, especially abroad, even though in reality it might not be the case. And so hostilities officially opened when the old *Enterprise* belonging to *Azzurra* consortium was rechristened *Italia*.

Victory '83, which Ian Howlett had designed for de Savary, was the best of the non-Australian yachts available at Newport at the end of 1983, and cooperation with the English proved to be an important element of the preparation carried out by the *Italia* consortium. Collecting and processing all the data for this new undertaking was done with Derek Clark and Graheme Winn as consultants; the latter had looked after the same sector in the English campaign of 1983, backed by Hewlett Packard.

When it came to the crew, many people felt that Italy simply did not have enough qualified yachtsmen to guarantee the quality offered by two consortiums. Italians who have won medals in their own country cannot be compared with Australians or Americans, or even put on a par with countries such as Great Britain and New Zealand, which are presenting one challenger each in 1987. What is lacking in Italy are people such as Conner, Kolius, Blackaller, Melges, Davis, Fogh, Cudmore and Cujot. Men who can sail boats fast and operate at the same time as active fund raisers.

At the beginning, the *Italia* consortium put the sports management in the hands of Lorenzo Bortolotti. He is one of the Italian skippers with the greatest experience in the IOR classes, and is manager of North sails in Italy. Flavio Scala was nominated helmsman. He had left the after-guard of *Azzurra* in the summer of 1983 following heated discussions. Together with Pelaschier, Scala was the only person with sufficient experience to guarantee being the helmsman of a 12-Metre.

The group began to train at Genoa and then in Sardinia. After only three months of tests, *Victory '83* won the 12-Metre world championship at Porto Cervo. Rod Davis and Mike Toppa were on *Victory*

Syndicate Chairman	ANGELO MONASSI
Design team	GIORGETTI & MAGRINI
Skipper	ALDO MIGLIACCIO
Helmsman	TOMMASO CHIEFFI
Names of boats	ITALIA 1, 2
Name of trial horse	VICTORY 83

'83 as well. Just as he had done in his IOR campaigns, Lorenzo Bortolotti called in American technicians in order to give him and his crew the best information, and undoubtedly this provided *Victory* with a feeling of security during regattas, a feeling that *Azzurra* just did not seem to have. *Azzurra* proved disappointing, and *Victory '83* triumphed. Cino Ricci said, 'This was not just an Italian victory. Let's see how we can do when we have to go it on our own'.

In designing the two new 12-Metre yachts on the programme, the Giorgetti & Magrini workshops started off with the idea 'that all research must start off completely from scratch'. The Australian experience that had led to victory at Newport showed that first of all, a correct working methodology was called for. Franco Giorgetti and Giorgio Magrini therefore set up a team, backed up by outside consultants as well. Raffaele Marazzi of Aermacchi and Michael Trimm of Intermarine were part of this group, together with technicians from the Institute of Naval Architecture at the Trieste Faculty of Engineering. Even though the design was based on the work done by Howlett for *Victory*, nothing was left to chance. In the first stage, the Italian group seemed to go along with what the English were doing. It was not so much a question of consultancy as much as one of 'international pollination' – the basis of all scientific progress in the world today.

Starting in 1984, the team from the Milanese workshop was working on a research programme to last two years. The first testing phase was carried out at Wageningen, with models on a 1:3 scale. The research continued then at the ship model basin at Trieste, with models on a 1:10 scale. The project for *Italia I* came about after the first ten months' work. She was built by Baglietto Shipyards at Varazze and launched in August 1985. Intermarine had concluded feasibility tests on building her in fibreglass, but the final choice was made in favour of light alloy. Just as had been done for *Australia II*, the results of the tests in the ship model basin were compared with a computerized flow pattern analysis developed by Aermacchi. Intermarine software was used for the drawing.

A first line-up was carried out in Sardinia by the group, with both *Italia I* and *Victory '83*. Rod David was there once again. Training started at the end of November at the Fremantle base. The logistics of the consortium impressed both local observers and international observers. Though the base seemed to be one of the best organized ones, the performances of *Italia I* and *Victory '83* were not so brilliant at the Mondiale '85. Here, Bortolotti was taking part as well, but as an adversary on board *Azzurra* and his role in the *Italia* consortium had been taken over by Aldo Migliaccio. Flavio Scala, Rod Davis and Paul Cayard were on board *Italia I*. Tommaso Chieffi and Albino Fravezzi were on *Victory '83*. The performance of the new 12-Metre seemed to stand up well, where speed was concerned, against others at the top of the lists. The problems connected with the Mondiale were not so much related to the boat as to the limited experience of the crew, and difficult conditions. Men fell overboard on two occasions. Despite the problems caused by her low freeboard, *Italia I* showed herself to be a good performer. As Giorgio Magrini said: 'The first *Italia* is a medium-to-light boat and with a large sail area'.

One thing definitely puts the Milanese workshop on a par with the great designers of the Mondiale '86, Briand and the New Zealander trio: the fact that none of them had ever designed a 12-Metre before. Indeed, the fact of having never worked for Newport no longer seems to be a necessary qualification. *Italia II* is being launched at the beginning of June. She is built of aluminium and is being constructed by Leghe Leggere Yacht of Fano. The second *Italia* consortium boat is being created thanks to the cooperation of G & M, Aermacchi, Intermarine. The design is more radical but not extreme – a coherent evolution following *Italia I*, but she will benefit from the results of the second stage of the research.

ABOVE: *a view of the entrance to Consorzio Italia's sailmaker's yard at Fremantle.*
RIGHT: *the enormous spinnaker of a 12-Metre laid out to dry occupies most of the courtyard outside the Italian base.*

Above: Italia II *virtually submerged after her disastrous launching at La Spezia; below, Franco Giorgetti and Giorgio Magrini, designers of* Italia *and* Italia II, *have recently opened an office in Australia: Giorgetti, Magrini & Williams.* Opposite: *the elegant main entrance to Casa Italia which will house a restaurant and syndicate offices.* Overleaf: *a spectacular photo of* Italia; *the skipper Aldo Migliaccio is the bearded man at the centre.*

CASA ITALIA

SECRET COVE YACHT CLUB
"CANADIAN AMERICA'S CUP CHALLENGE"

Canada mounted its first modern Cup challenge in 1983. Their 12-Metre, *Canada I*, was designed by the country's best known boat designer, and built in part by talent from its largest yacht builder. The Canadian syndicate had been heavily dependent on Canadian oil and timber money, and there was often not quite enough of it. The Canadians made a credible showing that summer, before falling to a faster *Australia II* and the better funded and prepared *Victory* from the United Kingdom. After the Cup was won, and people took stock of the situation, it was clear that Canada had the talent, the capability and the funds necessary for a serious Cup effort. They did not have the resources for two teams, but that is what they got when separate and antagonistic Canadian challenges were filed with the Royal Perth Yacht Club.

The 1983 challenge had been a good effort for Canada, but it had the ill-effect of stoking the regional conflicts within the country's industrial and sporting hierarchies. *Canada I* was a western boat, so it received little support from the eastern industrial center of the country. It was organized by a fly-by-night yacht club on the Pacific, so the establishment on the great lakes gave it less than full attention. When Don Green, a somewhat egocentric Ontario financier, announced the formation of the *True North* challenge, he fully expected the eastern establishment to follow in his wake. To a certain extent they did. Out west, the Secret Cove Yacht Club, the body that campaigned *Canada I* announced their intention to go all the way to Perth, and then watched in dismay as the price of oil began its long slippery slide, and the world demand for timber evaporated.

If the talent pool of world class sailors and designers in the United States is shallow, then it is microscopic in Canada. There is one Canadian designer of 12-Metres, Bruce Kirby, and he lives in the United States. There were no Canadian 12-Metre sailors five years ago, and only three or four people could claim any time at all on '12s'. When Green threw his hat in the ring, he immediately vacuumed up half the sailors, and much of the engineering talent. Steve Killing, who oversaw the construction of *Canada I* signed on as a designer, and Green extracted a deal with the Nova Scotia government to donate towards construction of the *True North* yachts.

Killing hired computer and aerodynamic talent, and before long Green proclaimed a breakthrough design. Soon production was underway, and the public relations men went wild. The KC–I team was swept away by a tidal wave of publicity. By the time they were underway with modifications of *Canada I*, as a prelude to building a new boat, many Canadians were convinced that they had already gone out of business. *True North* went into the water in early 1985, and the modified *Canada I* followed months later. By this time the sailing community was splitting into geographic camps more hostile than any California-New York rivalry in the United States, and the management of the two syndicates were savaging each other in the grim battle to corner funding. The Cup hopes of Canada were bleeding to death by the autumn of 1985.

The western boat raced against the Chicago team's *Clipper* in a frost-bound late November regatta. Melges and Jobson concurred that *Canada I* was the fastest '12' they ever sailed against. KC–1 was scheduled to go to San Francisco to meet the Golden Gate boat, and then take on *Eagle* and *Heart of America* syndicates while the new *Canada II* was under construction. At that time, the eastern boat was on its way to Fremantle and the 12-Metre world championships, which Green fully intended to win. By this time both syndicates were spending money that they did not have.

Bruce Kirby describes it as a period of 'terrible stop and go. Go ahead with the new design, then

Syndicate Chairman	MARVIN V. MACDILL
Designer	BRUCE KIRBY
Skipper	TERRY NEILSON
Names of boats	CANADA II, TRUE NORTH

stop when the money ran out. We were struggling along, making sure the crew was eating, but that was about all we did for a while'. Luckily for the Canadians, Kirby has always been an artist rather than a scientist and artists have smaller capital requirements. He began designing boats when he raced dinghies on the Great Lakes (Kirby was a member of the 1956 Canadian olympic team), and his test system consisted of taking the newest boat out racing. Later, he responded to a design request by doodling a boat on a sheet torn from a writing tablet. That design became the Laser, perhaps the most successful 'sit down' boat ever built. Kirby designed for the offshore racing community, and produced some cruising boats. All of them were much more the product of his imagination than of the test tank or computer analysis.

Kirby's modifications of *Canada I* grew out of his work on 6- and 8-Metre yachts. They were based on his experiences watching *Australia II* sail away from his '12' in Newport, and on the little bit of tank testing that could be done before the money stream dried up. It turned out that the original modifications were to be the last on the boat, for when the start day for the new design came, the syndicate was broke. Happily for Canada, the artist in Bruce triumphed mightily in the rebuild of *Canada I*. As a technical director of a rival sundicate put it, 'It looks to us as though Kirby found the right solution to the problems on his first try.' The danger to 'one-shot' designing, however, is that so many other solutions can never be explored.

Canada I was struggling in March and April, but *True North* was going under. The eastern team had bet heavily on success in Fremantle, presuming that victory would be the key to unlock the national treasuries. Instead, the boat barely made a ripple in the standings (two third places during the entire regatta) while plowing deep ditches through the budget. In the early spring of 1986, Green announced that he was mothballing the effort until someone came up with $US5,000,000. As it happened, there was some money about to be given to Canadian sailors, but they were the sailors aboard *Canada I*. Paul Phelon, a benefactor of the 1983 effort, pledged several million dollars to the western effort on the contingency that it become national. As a result *True North*, without the *True North* syndicate, was shipped from Nova Scotia to San Francisco to take part in the big testing regatta with the Americans. If *True North* proved faster than *Canada I*, then the westerners would crew her up, and take her to Australia instead of their own boat. As it happened, *Canada I* was significantly faster than the blue boat, and she proved very good against *Heart of America* as well. With these results on board, the Secret Cove Yacht Club officially renamed the rebuilt boat *Canada II*, and prepared to spend millions of new dollars on sails, equipment and support services for the Canadian challenge.

The bulk of their crew is from the *Canada I* team, since they have by far the happiest ship and the best organization. The boat's skipper, Terry Neilson, is the Finn bronze medalist from 1984, and is a former Laser world champion. Two important members of the *True North* crew jumped ship during the world championships, including their tactician, helping fill out the *Canada I* group, while technicians from the eastern team have proved very helpful in California.

The late influx of funds has given the Canadians the chance to create a first class sail inventory, significant back-up equipment, and a comfortable campaign budget. It came far too late for Kirby's new boat (the one that was supposed to be *Canada II*), but no one in the camp is complaining. Kirby says, 'Everyone tells us that our boat is the fastest thing around. And if they're right, then I shouldn't worry about going on to win the Cup. And just think of all the money we've saved by not building any more 12-Metre yachts.'

ABOVE: *Bruce Kirby, designer of* Canada I *(right), rechristened* Canada II *after a series of structural modifications.* Canada II *proved to be faster than* True North *during a series of tests which took place after the two Canadian teams joined forces, and was chosen to participate in the Louis Vuitton Cup.*

TRUE NORTH
CANADA

RIGHT: True North *when still contending for the Nova Scotia Yacht Squadron.*
ABOVE: *Canadian skipper Hans Fogh.*
LEFT: *Canadian crew lined up on board.*
OVERLEAF: True North. *After her disappointing performance in the 12-Metre championship, the* True North *syndicate was dissolved and its boat and part of the crew joined forces with the* Canada II *syndicate to form a single national challenge.*

12

RNSYS
12KC87
TRUE NORTH
CANADA

ROYAL NEW ZEALAND YACHT SQUADRON "R.N.Z. AMERICA'S CUP CHALLENGE TRUST"

Of all the dark horses galloping toward the America's Cup in 1987, New Zealand is surely the darkest. Like David facing up to Goliath, tiny New Zealand, with a population of about three million, has come up with a three-boat, $15 million challenge which is as audacious as it is professional. In New Zealand, where sailing is not so much a sport as a national obsession, the idea of challenging for and, why not, even winning the America's Cup, has fired the country's imagination. From Kaitaia, in the northernmost reaches of the North Island, to Invercargill (which is not so very far from Antarctica), everyone is pitching into a truly national effort.

When Alan Bond's *Australia II* won the America's Cup in 1983, all New Zealanders cheered the green and gold victory. Two who cheered loudest were Michael Fay and David Richwhite, the country's richest, most powerful merchant bankers. They decided then and there that they could win the Cup, too. Neither man was then encumbered with even the slightest knowledge of yachting, let alone interest in the sport. But that was beside the point. They had the kind of vision that shimmers in the mind's eye of only the most fantastic gamblers and dreamers. If they could do what Bond did, the entire New Zealand economy might bounce back in a Cup-led recovery!

Two and a half years later, and despite what must have been staggering odds, Fay found himself sitting in sweltering Fremantle, looking down on not one but two New Zealand '12s' and a boatyard swarming with brawny, sun-bronzed Kiwi sailors.

It was Fay who hit upon the brilliant idea of pooling the collective brain-power and resources of New Zealand's (and indeed the world's) top designers; Bruce Farr, Ron Holland and Laurie Davidson. Neither designer could have tackled such an enormous project alone and indeed not one of them would have wanted to go it alone.

Holland, Farr and Davidson held their first meeting in a London hotel and after inspecting the 300-ft-long tank testing facilities at the Wolfson Institute at the University of Southampton, decided to base their design analysis there rather than at the very much more expensive Netherlands Ship Model Basin where Ben Lexcen had developed his Cup winning winged keel concept and where the Australians and several of the challengers were already busily engaged on their own new design work. Further, New Zealand design testing was carried out at what the Kiwis refer to only as a secret European facility. Why are they keeping it a secret? According to Laurie Davidson, the facilities there (almost certainly in Italy) are believed to be far superior to the NSMB tank.

The designers' first move was to come up with two test models each at 1:10 scale. One of these was meant to represent *Victory '83* and the other, the Cup winner, *Australia II*. The New Zealanders admit that they acquired the lines of *Australia II* but they refuse to say from whom or under what circumstances that acquisition was made possible.

They built a total of five models and had the accuracy of their tank test data verified with computer analysis at NSMB. It was the fifth model, essentially a good heavy weather performer, which turned out to be their choice for the basis of the so-called 'plastic fantastics', the identical fibreglass '12s' that became *KZ–3* and *KZ–5* and which were both named *New Zealand*.

The New Zealanders were the first to produce fibreglass '12s'. After long, exhaustive and expensive consultations with Lloyds, the New Zealand hulls turned out to be exceptionally stiff. Laurie Davidson estimates they are something in the order of 20 times stiffer than aluminium 12-Metres. Because they are so very stiff, especially around the chain plate areas where the mast shrouds are attached, there is virtually no flexing. In theory, at least, this should give greater control over the entire

Syndicate President	AUSSIE MALCOLM
Designers	LAURIE DAVIDSON BRUCE FARR RON HOLLAND
Skipper	CHRIS DICKSON
Names of boats	NEW ZEALAND KZ-3, KZ-5, KZ-7

driving force of the rig. In practice, during the world championships however, the greater loads this brought to bear on the rig, which towers some 80ft above deck level, is believed to have been largely responsible for the loss of one mast and the severe damage sustained by another. The New Zealanders have now designed their own much more powerful three-spreader rigs which are being built by Australia's top mast-maker, Zapspar.

But *KZ–3* and *KZ–5* were never intended as anything other than full-size test beds and practice vehicles. The lessons they provided for the crews and the designers have helped shape *KZ–7*, the boat which ultimately carries New Zealand's hopes in the 1987 Cup showdown. The *KZ–7* design was finalized after a lot more testing and using 1:4 scale models for greater accuracy. Much of the keel design work was carried out on upside down models in wind tunnel facilities. One technique used smoke-like jets of vaporised kerosene to simulate water flow. Another used a combination of white paint and diesel oil which blew off in areas of laminar flow and was left clinging in areas of turbulence.

According to Laurie Davidson, they tried ten variations on the winged keel theme. 'Some of them were pretty way-out looking animals,' he said. 'Some had great big things on the bottom, some had little things on the bottom. Some even had two vertical elements. We've settled for what we call a hybrid. We think it works very well indeed.'

One of the key consultants in the keel design was found in, of all places, sleepy little Napier, a small town on the windy North Island. Richard Carn is a 30-year-old mechanical engineer whose speciality and great passion is windmills. Carn analysed all the keel data and in that area is regarded as an integral member of the design team. He also assisted in rudder design. Helmsman Chris Dickson was severely critical of the way the early rudders, essentially very deep IOR style devices, stalled out at large angles of helm which he often had to use during pre-start manoeuvres.

The New Zealanders believe they have made a 'giant leap forward' in the deck layout aboard *KZ–7*. 'We were very naive with the first two boats,' Davidson said. 'We stuck to a very conservative interpretation of the rules. Those cockpits were not the most efficient nor were they the most roomy in Fremantle for the worlds [championships].' The designers listened to crew suggestions and made a plywood mock-up in Fremantle in which every crewman had his own little niche virtually tailor-made to suit his particular needs. Now, instead of the cockpit simply being a big, shallow box with straight sides, *KZ–7* features cutaway sides about 450mm deep which provide much more volume and better angles for feet, a particularly important factor in the often boisterous weather off Fremantle. *KZ–7* has two cockpits instead of one as before. A bridge deck provides the division immediately in front of the helmsman's twin wheels. As on the 1983 Cup defender, *Liberty*, the tactician and navigator's stations are abaft the helm.

In *KZ–7*, the Kiwi design team have gone for a long boat (about 70ft) with little more sheer and a bow a little less severely knuckled than those aboard her predecessors. The lessons of the world series have clearly been learned. *KZ–7* is intended to be a good all-round boat, orientated toward the higher end of the wind range but also capable of taking care of herself in the light to moderate stuff as well.

Whatever becomes of the New Zealand challenge (and most experienced observers expect them to do exceedingly well with this their first effort) they have already earned top marks for sheer guts and determination, not to mention flair and sailing ability. Sometimes even the darkest horses triumph. Certainly, there will be many a sportsman around the world who will be rooting for the Kiwis. My guess is that they will not be disappointed.

KZ-3
NEW ZEALAND

ABOVE: *lowering the spinnaker aboard* New Zealand KZ 3. RIGHT: *young Chris Dickson, helmsman for New Zealand and one of the strongest match race specialists.* LEFT: New Zealand KZ 3, *sailing before the wind.*

ABOVE: New Zealand KZ 5 *sailing close to the wind. Both Royal New Zealand Yacht Club boats have fibreglass hulls.* BELOW: *view of the interior of the* New Zealand*'s sailmaker's yard in Australia.* OVERLEAF: *concentration on the faces of the* New Zealand*'s crew.*

NEW ZEALAND

NEW ZEALAN

KZ 3

The Defenders

Australia II *at the starting line*.

The Cup in Australia

On paper at least, four syndicates are seeking the right to defend the America's Cup on behalf of Royal Perth Yacht Club. In reality, however, there are at best, only two which because of the time and money and effort they have poured into it, genuinely deserve to be taken seriously. When the chips are finally down in Fremantle, no one doubts that it will be the Bond syndicate's *Australia IV* against the Parry syndicate's *Kookaburra III*. As harsh as that assessment may seem to all those who have put so much of their own time and money into this event, the painful truth is that the other defence contenders simply are not in the race. The Bond and Parry campaigns got under way almost as soon as the Cup was won. Their budgets, at $12 million and $16 million apiece, reflect the essential difference. Both the South Australian and the East Coast syndicates deserve top marks for trying but in both their cases it is a matter of too little, too late.

What this means is that with 14 international challengers, Royal Perth faces incredible odds against a successful defence. The best odds to be found in Australia in April 1986 were the 50:50 and these were being quoted by designer Ben Lexcen, a wonderfully cockeyed optimist if ever there was one.

It is a long shot, but what they lack in quantity, the Australians hope they may be able to make up for in quality. There is no doubt about it, the Bond and Parry campaigns are as formidable as they are financial. Bond has built two new boats, *Australia III* and *Australia IV*. *Australia III* showed how good she (and the Bond organization) was when she won the world championship series off Fremantle in February, 1986.

Starting way behind, Kevin Parry has given his designers, John Swarbrick, Iain Murray and Alan Payne, an unhindered commission to do whatever they have to to secure the defender's berth. Because they were so far behind, the Kookaburras have had to rely heavily on computer-based programmes. Some of the high-tech gear used aboard their boats came straight from the US and British aerospace and defence programmes where the crewmen who use it, ashore and aboard the racing yachts, were once employed.

It is out of the white heat of their great struggle with the Bond boats that Royal Perth is hoping a great defender will be forged. The two syndicates are headed by equally strong-willed and aggressive individuals, long on experience but sometimes short on tempers.

As the New York Yacht Club discovered all too painfully in 1983, the Aussies play rough indeed when the stakes are as high as the America's Cup. Having won the Cup in what often seemed like a no-holds-barred brawl, they apparently saw no reason for the fun to stop there. In the early months of 1985, when the Bond camp resolutely resisted any attempt by the Kookaburra crews to get alongside the bench-mark Cup winner, *Australia II*, there were wild scenes on Gage Roads which would have been familiar to the Barbary pirates. The battle, at that stage, was for credibility and the corporate funds that went with it. It was important for the Kookaburras to be seen to be winners, and not unnaturally the mostly young crews felt compelled to show off a little around the Bond guys. The feelings were reciprocated. Stickers went up around Fremantle: 'Stuff The Yellow Bird', they said. That slogan, not so much a threat as a full-blooded war cry, offered a wider public glimpse of the bitter private duel that had been raging between the Cup defence rivals. The result of all the water-born shenanigans was very nearly fatal. In the boisterous seas off Fremantle, high-powered tenders veered dangerously close to the bows of rival yachts, camera-toting spies trailed along in rubber duckies and there were stiffly worded notes and all manner of unprintable name calling.

The situation was such that Royal Perth was moved to issue a Memorandum to Defenders in which America's Cup Committee Chairman, Dr Stan Reid, laid down rules for rival defenders and warned them to behave themselves. Breaches would, he said, be viewed with the utmost seriousness by the committee.

Much to Royal Perth's relief, a sense of maturity soon crept into the proceedings. The *Kookaburra* camp settled into a very impressive campaign in which project manager, helmsman and co-designer Iain Murray gathered about him some of the country's finest sailors and technical people. The Bond camp had an obvious edge at the outset but it was Murray, through sheer dedication and not a little help from Kevin Parry's chequebook, who gradually reduced the gap to a point where, on the eve of their confrontation, it could be said that the two camps were virtually at level pegging. The fact that that recognition came from within the Bond camp was in itself as strong an indicator as there could be that we were going to see some fine racing from the Australians in the summer of 1986–87.

The initial skirmishes were, if not forgotten, then pushed into the background as the two camps, under the watchful eye of the Royal Perth Race Committee, settled down to solid trial sessions that included rigorous pre-start practice, short, sharp tacking duels and close encounters at mark roundings. To veteran observers there appeared to be very little in it.

The only point at which the Australian defence in general and the *Kookaburra* campaign in particular might have been said to have stumbled, came when the Parry camp decided not to enter the world 12-Metre championships off Fremantle in February 1986. The *Kookaburra* camp remained convinced that the International Yacht Racing Union would not change its mind on making public the hitherto secret details contained on rating certificates. Because they did not wish to jeopardize the millions of dollars they had spent in tank testing and developing what they believed were particularly fast hull shapes, the decision was made not to complete. No less a judge than *Australia II*'s Cup-winning helmsman, John Bertrand, said he believed the stay-away tactics cost *Kookaburra*, in effect, six months in terms of lost experience and something like $5 million in potential sponsorships had they and not *Australia III*, won the regatta. The fact that the IYRU reversed its policy only after it was too late for *Kookaburra* to officially enter, made the situation even more frustrating than it had been.

Instead, Iain Murray and his boys made the best of it by embarking on extensive changes to *Kookaburra I*'s underwater shape. They were changes which have subsequently shown to have improved the boat dramatically.

Both Bond and Parry have had built new boats and unless they show themselves to be utter duds (and that is very definitely not on the cards) it will almost certainly be *Australia IV* and *Kookaburra III* which compete for the defence. As much as one might wish to see exceptional performances from South Australia and the East Coast boat, that prospect seems remote in the extreme.

The eventual defender will choose herself over four months of rigorous racing and whether she does or does not retain the Cup she will have been through an unprecedented three years of preparation for an event, the likes of which the sporting world will be privileged to watch.

AUSTRALIA

ROYAL PERTH YACHT CLUB
AUSTRALIA'S DEFENCE 1987 LIMITED
"BOND SYNDICATE"

During the 1983 America's Cup campaign, Ben Lexcen was often tormented by a recurring dream in which, having won the Cup, he went to sleep cradling it in his arms only to wake and find it gone.

Three years later, Lexcen is still visited by the same eerie nightmare. Knowing the obsessive, some would say paranoic, nature of America's Cup competition, the nightmare's reappearance is scarcely surprising. Lexcen, the brilliant designer whose radical winged keel revolutionized the 12-Metre world and brought him international fame, is still very much a prisoner of the Cup he once thought would set him free. In 1986–87, Lexcen is again the lynch-pin in the Bond syndicate's bid to retain the Cup it won in that historic series in Newport. No sooner was that campaign over than Lexcen, the man who had created in *Australia II* the fastest 12-Metre yacht in the world, set off again in pursuit of still more speed. He had always maintained that although *Australia II*'s winged keel was fast, her canoe shaped hull was, to use his own super-critical assessment, 'slow'.

He was certain that given time he never had in 1983, he could come up with a much, much faster hull and very much faster winged keels. He already knew where the changes ought to be made and after only the most preliminary testing he came up with the lines of what were to become *Australia III* and *South Australia*, virtually identical sister ships in hull form and initial keel shape.

Australia III went to the Bond camp while the royal blue *South Australia* went to the Adelaide-based *South Australia* syndicate headed by America's Cup veteran, Sir James Hardy.

Although she was carefully shrouded from the moment she rolled out of builder Steve Ward's shed, *Australia III* obviously had more freeboard and more volume in her ends than her predecessor which was of course designed specifically for the generally light airs and relatively smooth seas off Newport, Rhode Island. The winds and seas off Fremantle demand a much more powerful hull form and certainly *Australia III* does have a very impressive speed and motion in these conditions.

At the beginning of 1986, she sailed so consistently well that she was able to win the 12-Metre world championships in just six of the seven races. The Bond syndicate decided, for their own good political reasons, not to enter her in the seventh.

Throughout that series, *Australia II*, which came third behind the New Zealand boat, *KZ–5*, also showed that despite the adverse conditions, she was still one of the world's best. The Bond syndicate is extremely fortunate in having some of Australia's most experienced yachtsmen in a very aggressive two-boat programme. *Australia II* and *Australia III* are sailed by separate crews under 27-year-old Colin Beashel (the 12-Metre world title holder) and Gordon Lucas. Both crews go hard at it as if their team-mates were in fact their deadliest enemies. The result has been a keen, competitive edge, honed day after day, six days a week, practically every week since January 1985, in relentless match race trials. The America's Cup has never seen a defence effort even remotely like it.

Inside the waterfront headquarters are the powerful Data General computers which are in many ways the heart of the entire operation. Glen Read, the computer-whizz from Data General who played such a vital role for the *Australia II* campaign in 1983 is once again with the Bond defence effort in Fremantle. His main frame computers here are collecting, analysing and storing ten times the amount of data *Australia II* collected in Newport. Computers on board the racing yachts are linked up with monitors and recorders on board the tenders. Analysis takes place ashore with the aid of the main frame computer.

If the computer room is the nerve centre of the Bond syndicate's operations, that is very largely because it also houses the assorted multi-coloured electronics of weather expert Roger 'Clouds'

Syndicate Chairman	ALAN BOND
Designer	BEN LEXCEN
Helmsmen	COLIN BEASHEL GORDON LUCAS

Badham. Badham is an extremely talented meterologist who has a special knack with computers. He takes a continuous stream of raw data on wind strength, air and water temperature, wave height and frequency and boils it all down to succinct 20 to 30 minute briefings for the racing crews each day. Badham has become so adept at his analysis that he is said to be right 90 per cent of the time in predicting the time, direction and strength of wind shifts on the Cup course.

The maintenance workshops adjacent to the headquarters building are fitted with the latest engineering devices that quickly allow fabrication of even the most sophisticated parts on the spot. Steve Harris, the bearded and perpetually grimy maintenance boss, remains the tower of strength he was to the 1983 campaign. Not far from the maintenance area and still within the high-walled Bond compound is the sail loft, a huge expanse of varnished plywood so big that a 12-Metre mainsail can be easily recut. Early in 1986, the Bond syndicate lost nearly $300,000 worth of sails when fire, caused by an electrical fault, swept through a storage container not far from the loft. Unfortunately, many of the sails were damaged beyond repair, included the bench-mark gear used by *Australia II* in winning the Cup. That setback was one of a number to plague the Bond camp's early defence efforts. Two masts were severely damaged in embarrassing dockyard accidents.

One of the major aces up the Bond syndicate's sleeve is Tom Schnackenberg, the moustachioed New Zealander (now a resident Australian) who designed all *Australia II*'s Cup-winning sails in 1983. Schnackenberg, a former nuclear physicist and now one of the leading lights in the North Sails empire, is working on new and improved sail shapes which, it is hoped, will once again help make the difference. Continuity is an important theme within the Bond camp. At least two-thirds of the original Cup winning team, including the racing crew and the shoreside back-up staff, remain together and just as committed to another successful campaign. John Bertrand is the notable exception. Bertrand has made it clear he will not steer the boat in 1986–87 but will act as an adviser and syndicate director.

These days the America's Cup is said to be not so much a boat race as a battle between shoreside organizations. If that is true, then the Bond camp is in very good shape indeed. Warren Jones, the self-styled 'corporate brawler' whose aggressive no-nonsense style did so much to keep the New York Yacht Club back-peddling during the great keel row in 1983 is once again organizing the entire Bond effort as its executive director. On the wall in Jones' office is an enormous flow-chart in which every day leading up to the Cup defence is accounted for in minute detail. In the slot for February, 1987 is the inscription 'WIN THE CUP'. That is no idle boast. Although Lexcen and Jones and Bond concede that the chances of Australia hanging onto the Cup are no better than 50:50, there remains a solid core of well-founded confidence.

In April 1986, Lexcen finally froze his design for *Australia IV*, the second new '12' for the Bond syndicate. Lofting started almost immediately although work on keel shapes was expected to continue right up until, and perhaps even including, the elimination trials. *Australia IV* was expected to be over seven feet longer than *Australia II* with slightly more volume in the ends than *Australia III* and several unusual and innovative features.

Lexcen, who has been orchestrating his own spying operations, particularly on the new American '12s', was being extremely cautious in keeping his own plans for the new boat secret. *Australia IV*, he said, would be very different and very much faster than *Australia III*. He predicted she would be an astonishing four minutes faster around the 24.5-mile Cup course in moderate winds than *Australia II*. If that bold prediction is true, then perhaps his nightmare will eventually go away.

ABOVE: *the famous winged keel of* Australia II. RIGHT: Australia III *the Royal Perth Yacht Club 12-Metre that won the 1986 world championship.*

AUSTRALIA III

ABOVE: Australia II, *the yacht that won the America's Cup in 1983.* RIGHT: *from left to right, Tom Schnackenberg, sailmaker; John Longley, operations manager; Ben Lexcen, designer for the Bond syndicate.*

AUSTRALIA III
Royal Perth Yacht Club
Fremantle
AUSTRALIA III

ABOVE: *the Australian crew returning after a day's training session.* LEFT: Australia III *sailing close to the wind.* OVERLEAF: *the crew prepares for a manoeuvre.*

KOOKABURRA

ROYAL PERTH YACHT CLUB TASKFORCE 1987 LIMITED "KOOKABURRA SYNDICATE"

To most Australians, the kookaburra and its joyous, almost hysterical, cackling laughter, is about as identifiably Aussie as the blood red of Ayres Rock at sunset or the overpowering eucalyptus aroma of native gum trees in the noon-day heat. It was, therefore, a powerful, evocative symbol, wisely chosen by Kevin Parry's Task Force '87 syndicate to adorn the transoms of the three '12s' that bear the wild bird's name; kookaburras can be fearless and particularly aggressive carnivores but it is within the laugh that we find the bird's true symbolism for Parry. So what if it costs him $16.1 million (and by mid-April 1986 it had). By hook or by crook, Parry, the Perth multi-millionaire businessman, aims to have the last laugh on his great rival, Alan Bond, when it comes to defending the America's Cup.

Bond and Parry both live in Perth and are both extraordinarily successful in quite separate business endeavours. The two men scarcely know each other and yet both share the same passionate belief in their ability to defend the America's Cup. In a not so subtle way, often characteristic of self-made men, Bond and Parry behaved a bit like Punch and Judy in the early stages of their Cup defence campaigns. They did not actually hit each other over the head but there were plenty of verbal punches thrown and not a little bitterness generated in the process.

Kevin Parry deserves special praise (or is it pity?) for having started with nothing but an idea, fierce determination and an awful lot of money, and creating a three-boat campaign at least the equal of anything else being put together anywhere in the world. Parry deserves that special praise not least because he is not a yachtie. A former baseball star and a stink-potter to boot, he cheerfully admits that he can barely discern the sharp end from the blunt end let alone tell you which of two boats happen to be in the lead at any given moment on a windward leg. His Cup involvement began almost by accident.

When Alan Bond came home to Perth after *Australia II*'s great Cup win in September 1983 and suddenly found himself lumbered with the staggering burden of defending it, he looked around for support and got very little. Australians, especially at the big money corporate level, seemed quite prepared to bask in the glory of *Australia II*'s win but were, thereafter, not too interested in paying to keep the Cup safely in Perth. Bond met Parry at a businessman's luncheon and some of his enthusiasm rubbed off. Parry remembers thinking, 'yeah, I'd like to have a go at that'. He got some fellows to draw up preliminary ideas of what it might cost. When they told him $5 million to $6 million he says he figured he would have no trouble at all in paring that down to $4.5 million. By April 1986, Parry's tilt at the auld mug had turned into a three-boat, $16.1-million monster. It is just as well he loves every minute of it.

Kevin Parry is a short, blocky, balding bear of a man who, after starting with virtually nothing (he and his father made furniture in a ricketty old backyard factory) is now into retailing, real estate, oil and minerals and high-tech video softwear and laser discs and submarine technology. Having made his own fortune, he possesses the vision and the clout essential to seize the Cup and of course the opportunities it presents to expand his business operations even further.

One of Parry's first and probably most significant America's Cup decision was to appoint 27-year-old Iain Murray as helmsman, project director and co-designer. Murray, one of the finest yachtsmen in the world, is a natural, seat-of-the-pants sailor who also happens to understand the enormous benefits to be derived from computer technology in design and everything else that makes boats go faster and faster these days.

Murray's special interest in computers was just as well because it showed him a way to help bridge the enormous experience gap that yawned between the Parry syndicate's fledgling efforts and the ultra-sophisticated campaign being waged by the Bond

Syndicate Chairman	KEVIN PARRY
Designers	JOHN SWARBRICK IAIN MURRAY
Skipper	IAIN MURRAY
Helmsman	GRAHAM FREEMAN

camp. Murray gathered about him some of the best computer brains in the world. Chris Todter came from the United States where he had worked in the aerospace and defence industries on things like navigational guidance systems for missiles and supersonic jet aircraft. Derek Clark came from the United Kingdom where he had a background in engineering and electronics as well as extensive experience in 12-Metres. It was Clark who conceived the brilliant idea for the rule-cheating bendy mast first worn by the British Cup challenger, *Lionheart*, in 1980.

Together, Todter and Clark evolved exceptionally accurate computer performance monitoring gear housed below decks in watertight plexiglass cases aboard all three *Kookaburra*s. It is just behind the helmsman that the navigator (or technician as he tends to be called these days) sits at a raised, circular pod which incorporates the video display terminal. It is this computer brain, effectively the twelfth man in the crew, which sets the *Kookaburra*s apart from virtually every other 12-Metre. The computer monitors and records a host of critical performance functions which have been able to give Murray an excellent idea of his rapid progress up the learning curve. The *Kookaburra* computers are interfaced with other gear aboard their tender and at the end of a day's racing it is all transferred to the main frame stored at the Task Force '87 headquarters in Fremantle. The *Kookaburra* computers, said to be 100 times more powerful than those used so successfully aboard *Australia II* in Newport, are capable of logging a staggering 10 megabytes of data – one million characters – each day. Its final analysis boils down to a daily analysis of between 20 and 30 printed pages of tables and statistics that chart the highs and lows of the day's performance. Murray is convinced that the data has been of tremendous assistance in pushing *Kookaburra III* so close to *Australia IV*.

Murray is the first to admit, however, that he would have been nowhere as close had he not purloined (his term) Ben Lexcen's plans for *Australia II*. He will not say where he got the plans, only that they became available and he had no hesitation in snapping them up. One suspects that there were many other designers around the world who did precisely the same thing when they started off their own design programmes for 1987. *Australia II* was after all the bench-mark against which all the other contenders had to be judged. But having started with *Australia II*, Murray poured many of his own innovative design ideas into the *Kookaburras*. John Swarbrick, a young Perth naval architect was engaged to do all the formal testing and evaluation and later the Cup veteran, Alan Payne, was called in to work exclusively on winged keel shapes in test facilities in Melbourne and in Launceston, in northern Tasmania.

The beautiful irridescent gold-painted *Kookaburra*s display a racy elegance that certainly sets them apart from the other Australian '12s'. The boats are distinguished by more freeboard than *Australia II* and feature long, graceful overhangs, especially their transoms which tend to be shallow, shield-shapes which help give the boats longer effective waterline length when they are heeled at sea. Murray points to the overhangs as the main distinguishing features between *Australia II* and the *Kookaburra*s.

It is Murray's firm belief that the *Kookaburra* designs do represent something of a design breakthrough and because of that he has gone to extraordinary lengths to protect them. Like the Bond syndicate and the *America II* syndicate, the *Kookaburra*s are kept secure in their own submarine pens, which are sealed with heavy aluminium doors and are open only to the sky. *Kookaburras*' back up facilities are probably the best in Fremantle. They have their own huge sail loft and workshop as well as their own private shed where the yachts can be hauled out for major surgery or repairs. Kevin Parry wants the last laugh on Alan Bond and *Kookaburra* may give him precisely that.

ABOVE: *John Swarbrick and Iain Murray (right), the designers of the* Task Force *syndicate's two 12-Metre yachts.* RIGHT: Kookaburra I *and* II *on a training session.*

ABOVE: *the two* Kookaburra *yachts in action. The navigator of the yacht in the foreground is operating a computer.* OPPOSITE: *training Task Force syndicate vessels.*

12
KA-11
12
KA 11

ABOVE: Kookaburra.
RIGHT: Kookaburra *syndicate flags bearing the image of the aggressive and rare Australian bird from which the yachts take their name.* OVERLEAF: Kookaburra, *slack on the Indian Ocean in light winds.*

KOOKABURRA

SOUTH AUSTRALIA

ROYAL SOUTHERN YACHT SQUADRON "SOUTH AUSTRALIA SYNDICATE"

In the midst of the green and gold euphoria that swirled around *Australia II*'s America's Cup win, no less than eight separate Australian syndicates were formed to help defend the Cup. Four of those syndicates, from Victoria, Queensland, Tasmania and Western Australia quickly realized that there was something more to a successful Cup defence than mere hoopla. Money, lots and lots of hard cash, was required and those syndicates simply did not have it. In those early months there were those who felt confident that the South Australian syndicate would go the same way. Those who did so reckoned without the sheer guts and determination of the South Australians. With virtually no background in 12-Metres, save for syndicate chief, Sir James Hardy (who has, of course, campaigned previous Australian challengers), they set about creating a one-boat campaign which soon became an integral part of the overall defence. No one seriously expects South Australia to be the actual Cup defender. That is not a reflection on the boat, her crew or her sails, but rather a simple matter of experience, time and money that they did not have.

South Australia is virtually a sister ship to *Australia III*. She was designed by Ben Lexcen after tank testing at the Netherlands Ship Model Basin. In theory, at least, she should be as fast as *Australia III*. Anyone who saw the performance difference between the two boats at the world championship series might be excused for assuming they were utterly dissimilar designs. *Australia III* won the world title while *South Australia* came home a disappointing eighth.

When *South Australia* first went on the water she showed herself to be exceptionally fast in light air. On many occasions she was able to beat *Australia II*, the boat acknowledged as perhaps the fastest light air flier in the world. But since there is not a lot of light air in Fremantle the South Australians decided on major underwater surgery and a re-ballasting that optimised the boat's moderate to heavy air ability. A completely new winged keel was designed by Lexcen. The new keel was so different that much of the boat's bottom had to be cut away and rebuilt. The changes killed her light air ability but sent her speed up with *Australia II* and *III* in the moderate stuff. The South Australian campaign has a budget of only $7 million so they have had to be extremely careful with cash outlays. That has not, however, stopped them ordering two new masts, one from Sparcraft and the other from Zapspar.

South Australia's crew are drawn from all the Australian states. And although the final 11 were to be chosen in October, aspirants have been subjecting themselves to a rigorous commando-style exercise regime organized by the South Australian Sports Institute. *South Australia*'s helmsman is Fred Neill who has had a distinguished record in Australian Admiral's Cup and Clipper Cup teams. Although Neill lacks top-flight match-race experience, his natural ability at the helm and his great stamina virtually guarantee him a helmsman's berth. The other helmsman is a young Sydney skipper, Phil Thompson, who, over a number of

Syndicate Chairman	GRAHAM G. SPURLING E.D.
Designer	BEN LEXCEN
Skipper	JOHN SAVAGE
Helmsman	PHIL THOMPSON

years, has distinguished himself in Etchells and Solings.

Thompson joined the South Australian camp after the world series and his presence immediately made a big difference on the boat. Sir James Hardy still serves as a reserve helmsman but is now likely to take a more active shore-side advisory role. Hardy has never doubted that the *South Australia* syndicate has the right stuff. 'I think we have a bit more all-round capability than *Australia II*,' he said. 'I do have a nice feeling about the boat and that's important. From the moment I stepped aboard her she felt right. All the really great boats have that special quality. The fact that we've got a real cloud of sail aloft makes all the difference.' In fact, *South Australia* has a lot more sail area than *Australia II*. Her boom is about 18in longer and that means she must be carrying about 200sq ft more sail. The mainsail roach is so round that Lexcen was forced to design a short bumpkin to get her backstay outboard.

The South Australian syndicate paid the Bond syndicate $600,000 for the Lexcen design. The deal allowed them to be given a certain amount of administrative help but no computer data. This understandably led to more than a little resentment among the South Australians, many of whom thought they were being used by the Bond group in much the same way that the Victorian-based *Challenge 12* campaign was used by the *Australia II* outfit back in 1983.

'The blokes sometimes got a bit cranky because they felt Bondy was just using them up,' Hardy said. 'Well, that's the very pressure you get in an America's Cup.

'In the past I think Australians have tended to regard the America's Cup as a bit of a silver spoon job, something that really wasn't all that important. Now, people do realize that the Cup is the top. It's a symbol of tremendous national pride not only to the Americans but to all those who compete for it. I think that message has filtered down to Aussie yachtsmen.'

So can *South Australia* retain the Cup? 'I think *South Australia* will play a crucial role in the Cup defence,' he said. 'I am not going to say that we will necessarily be the defender but I am convinced that our role will count for a lot in the final analysis. I think all South Australians will be proud of the effort we have put in. Yes, I think Australia can retain the Cup. I'm scared of our defence above the water but I'm not at all worried about our defence below the water. Ben Lexcen has come up with hulls which are every bit as good as the opposition. The fear I do have is all the technology they have to throw at us. When you start to translate that into spars and rigging and especially sail fabric and then add up their match-racing ability, you start to shake at the knees a bit.'

Hardy believes the Australian defenders will have a decided home town advantage. 'We are down under,' he said. 'I've heard the Americans and others talk about that in almost awestruck terms. The fact that we are playing on our home paddock, that's our trump card.'

SOUTH AUSTRALIA
KA 6
PORT ADELAIDE
R.S.A.Y.S.

ABOVE AND LEFT: South Australia, *the 12-Metre from Adelaide, designed by Ben Lexcen who is involved with the Bond syndicate.* BELOW: *Jim Hardy, prominent member of the South Australian group.*

ABOVE: South Australia *sailing close to the wind on a training session*. BELOW: *a syndicate lorry bearing the official colours and the name of the chief sponsor*. OVERLEAF: *the Adelaide challenger in the 1986 world championship*.

12
KA8
Major Sponsor
MITSUBISHI
MOTORS AUSTRALIA LTD.
COMBO

STEAKIDNEY

ROYAL SYDNEY YACHT SQUADRON "THE EASTERN AUSTRALIA DEFENCE SYNDICATE"

Australia's America's Cup Cinderella, the East Coast syndicate 12-Metre that rejoices in the most unlikely name, *Sunshine*, emerged late in April and only just in time for the ball. Peter Cole's lovely, all white hull, arguably the best looking of all the current Cup defenders, was meant to have been launched five months before. Difficulties of one sort or another kept postponing her debut. In retrospect, that may not have been such a terribly bad thing. The postponements allowed Cole, one of Australia's most gifted designers, the luxury of extended refinement over 12 solid months. The final design, the product of 22 hull shapes and 11 winged keel variations, tested exceptionally fast in moderate to heavy conditions simulated in the Netherlands Ship Model Basin in Wageningen.

The quiet and unassuming Cole, who has no formal training in naval architecture, but who does have a great natural flair for design, was confident that his numbers were right. He has given the boat exceptionally powerful U-shaped sections amidships with plenty of volume in the ends, characteristics regarded as essential in coping with Fremantle's notoriously boisterous winds and seas. Under the complex 12-Metre formulae, such a powerful hull-form is usually associated with a corresponding sail area penalty but Cole has been so clever in avoiding this that his boat carries very nearly maximum sail area. She is, in fact, only one foot short of maximum on her J measurement. The sharply knuckled bow is however extremely fine and almost knife-like while the stern sections flatten out on a very long run to a shallow vee-shaped counter. The total effect is of a long, mean-looking '12', quite unlike her Australian rivals and yet not too far different in blood lines from the fastest of the American and European '12s'. She looks not unlike *French Kiss* minus her distinctive sheer. Deck layout is fairly conventional although once again very carefully thought out. Aloft, however, Cole has gone for a beautifully clean although extremely strong looking triple-spreader rig. Whatever else happens, the mast is unlikely to fall out of the boat.

The delaying gremlins that plagued the yachts

Syndicate Chairman	SYD FISCHER
Designer	PETER COLE
Skipper	GARY SHEARD

construction did not go away after her launch. On April 21, when she was unveiled for the media's benefit in the shadow of the fantastic soaring white sails of Sydney's Opera House, the boat was far from finished. It took a further three weeks before she was ready for her first sea trials against *Australia* (the 1980 Cup challenger) in the Pacific off Sydney. On her first outing, the new boat (somehow I just cannot bring myself to call her *Sunshine*!) proved exceptionally fast in the five- to 15-knot winds and relatively smooth seas. She was much more manoeuverable than *Australia* and showed a dramatic accelerating quality. After the two '12s' started parallel and two boatlengths apart, the new boat was able to forge ahead three boatlengths and climb comfortably to windward of *Australia* in just eight minutes. Her downwind speed was equally impressive and she was able to slide away from *Australia* on both reaches and runs.

But a fast boat, as many before have come to learn, is only part of the equation, and with so many of Australia's star yachtsmen already committed to the three rival America's Cup camps, it has not been easy attracting top talent. The East Coast syndicate was therefore forced to recognize the ancient economic principle that in a market place, scarce resources command a very high price. If you want those resources, in this case experience and sheer sailing ability, you have to haul out the cheque book and pay big bucks.

The East Coast syndicate is very fortunate to have secured the considerable talent of Sydney's top sailmaker, Bob Fraser. Fraser and computer whizz Brad Stephens have written their own design programme and have had outstanding success in many of the hot fractional-rig classes raced in Sydney.

Having failed to raise enough money from the corporate sector, the syndicate has renamed the boat *Steakidney* (to rhyme with Sydney) in the hope that Australians might embrace a people's boat, but whether the gamble will pay off remains to be seen. Meanwhile, it must be hard for Pete Cole to see his beautiful boat held up to ridicule, as a PR group scrabbles around to raise money.

LEFT: *the crew of* Sunshine *lined up on deck on launching day*. ABOVE: *the defender and her trial horse*. OPPOSITE: *the yacht that will attempt to defend the Royal Perth Yacht Club colours, training in Syndey Bay together with* Australia, *the 12-Metre that competed in the 1980 challenge*. OVERLEAF: Sunshine *against the Sydney skyline*.

KA·14
KA·14
NewsPlus
NEWSAGENT

STEAKIDNEY

The Louis Vuitton Cup: the challenger that wins this cup is automatically given the right to stake her claim to the America's Cup.

Appendices

THE ASSIGNMENT BY THE NEW YORK YACHT CLUB OF THE AMERICA'S CUP AND ITS ACCEPTANCE BY THE ROYAL PERTH YACHT CLUB, DATED 27th SEPTEMBER 1983

This Assignment and Acceptance is made as of the 27th day of September 1983, by and between the New York Yacht Club (the 'NYYC') and the Royal Perth Yacht Club of Western Australia ('RPYC').

The yacht AUSTRALIA II, as representative of the RPYC, having won the America's Cup (the 'Cup') in accordance with the terms and conditions of a deed of gift dated October 24, 1887, between George L. Schuyler and the NYYC, as amended by an order of the Supreme Court of the State of New York dated December 17, 1956 and as interpreted by resolution adopted by the Board of Trustees of the NYYC on March 27, 1958 and by resolutions adopted by the Board of Trustees of the NYYC on July 15, 1980 and amended on March 9, 1982, and the Footnotes in Amplification thereof published by the NYYC, such deed of gift as so amended and interpreted herein referred to as the 'Deed of Gift', the parties hereto agree that:

1. *Assignment.* The NYYC hereby assigns and transfers the Cup to the RPYC on the condition that the RPYC shll hold the Cup, in trust, in accordance with the terms and conditions of the Deed of Gift.

2. *Acceptance.* The RPYC hereby accepts the Cup subject to the said trust and to the terms and conditions of the Deed of Gift and covenants that:

(a) It will faithfully and fully see that the conditions of the Deed of Gift are fully observed and complied with by any contestant for the Cup during the holding thereof by it; and

(b) It will assign, transfer and deliver the Cup to the foreign yacht club whose representative yacht shall have won the same in accordance with the terms and conditions of the Deed of Gift, provided that said foreign yacht club shall, by instrument in writing lawfully executed, enter with the RPYC into the like covenants as are herein entered into by it, such instrument to contain a like provision for the successive assignees to enter into the same covenants with their respective assignors, and such instrument to be executed in duplicate, with one counterpart to be retained by each club and a copy thereof to be forwarded to the NYYC.

3. *Applicable Law.* The parties hereto further agree that, the trust under which the Cup is held having been created under the laws of the State of New York, and having been amended as aforesaid by order of the Supreme Court of the State of New York, the terms and conditions of the Deed of Gift shall be governed by, and construed in accordance with, such laws, and any proceeding for the amendment or interpretation of such terms and conditions shall be brought before the courts of the State of New York.

IN WITNESS THEREOF, the parties have caused this instrument to be executed by their duly authorised officers at the date first above written.

NEW YORK YACHT CLUB
by Robert G. Stone Jr.
Commodore

ROYAL PERTH YACHT CLUB OF WESTERN AUSTRALIA (INC.)
by P.R. Dalziell
Commodore

Challenger of Record

The Deed of Gift lies at the heart of the America's Cup series. This act of donation marks the occasion of George L Schuyler's presentation of the Cup in 1887, originally won by the yacht *America* at Cowes in 1851, to the New York Yacht Club . . . 'upon the condition that it shall be preserved as a perpetual Challenge Cup for friendly competition between foreign countries.' The Deed then goes on to specify that 'Any organized Yacht Club of a foreign country, incorporated, patented, or licensed by the legislature . . . shall always be entitled to the right of sailing a match for this Cup . . .'

As it turned out, for the next 100 years of its existence, the America's Cup was a private affair between two yacht clubs: only one challenger and the New York Yacht Club as the sole defender. Subsequently, representatives from both parties, after a succession of visits on either side and a dearth of correspondence, got together to lay down, sign and seal the conditions governing the races.

Although there was still only one challenger for the 1964 and 1967 Cup series – the Royal Thames Yacht Club and the Royal Sydney Yacht Squadron respectively – in the 1970 edition the New York Yacht Club received notices of challenge from the Royal Sydney Yacht Squadron, the Royal Dorset Yacht Club, the Yacht Club D'Hyères and the Royal Yacht Club of Greece. It was on this occasion that the possibility of organizing elimination races in Newport was first looked into. The New York Yacht Club proceeded to negotiate the conditions for future cup matches with, as tradition dictated, the Royal Sydney Yacht Squadron (whose proposal of candidature had been the first to arrive) but a new clause was inserted in the final written agreement which conceded the substitution of the challenging club at the end of the selection procedure.

In 1970, in Newport, only two groups, the Australian and French syndicates, actually presented themselves and their representative yachts *Gretel* and *France*. For the first time in the history of the America's Cup, a proposal was made to organize official trial regattas between challenging parties. Two years later, a total of seven challenges were made and the terms were stipulated by the Royal Thames Yacht Club (referred to as 'the challenger of record' by Douglas Philips-Burt in his book *The Cumberland Fleet*) which managed to draw a concession from the New York Yacht Club in the form of two important provisions: an International Jury and a Rules Committee composed of three measures. Thus, the Royal Thames, although it did not enter a craft, presided over the selection trials between *Southern Cross* and *France*. The concept of the 'Challenger of Record' had now been officially introduced, if not completely standardized, and its mediatory role between the challenging and defending parties for a correct and just competitive system assumed ever-increasing importance.

As from 1974, the Challenger of the Record has been the Club that officially represents all eligible contestants; it is the Club that signs the conditions for the holding of the final Cup race and which coordinates the various phases of selection.

Clearly, this is no easy task. In fact, it is always the club that defends the Cup that disposes of the greatest power. It is the authority that accepts the notices of challenge, that liberally nominates the Challenger of Record and lays down the basic conditions governing the races. In practice, the defending club also has the power to veto proposals put forward by the challengers as to the selection procedure. Thus, acceptance of this nomination can mean weeks of gruelling mediation since it is the responsibility of that body which establishes the conditions to obtain best guarantees for what we term 'fair racing'.

The Royal Perth Yacht Club has nominated the Yacht Club Costa Smeralda as Challenger of Record for the 1987 edition, being the first to have submitted a notice of challenge. However, this was not the sole motivation for its choosing. There is no doubt that the Porto Cervo club has had considerable experience in the organization of international regattas, not least the Sardinia Cup (held biennially) and the world 12-Metre championships, last held in 1984. Graeme Owens (member of the RPYC and an IYRU judge) together with Noel Robbins (executive manager of the America's Cup Committee of the Royal Perth Yacht Club) and Gianfranco Alberini (Commodore of the Yacht Club Costa Smeralda) have been elected to coordinate negotiations for the drafting of conditions for the 1987 Cup races.

During a series of meetings held in Bermuda, Porto Cervo, London, Newport and Perth, in which representatives of all clubs and unions interested in selection took part, Gianfranco Alberini supervised and moderated the talks, sometimes beset with heated altercations, which were instrumental in defining the formalities governing the elimination series. These trials have as their purpose 'the preparation and selection of the best yacht for the America's Cup Match'. The French firm Louis Vuitton, which gave its support to the challenging parties in 1983, has renewed its sponsorship so that the challengers races have now become The Louis Vuitton Cup.

Never before have challenging clubs been allowed to participate to such an extent in the negotiation and drafting of the regulations governing the races. The challengers originally entered by Royal Perth numbered 24. Consequently, one of the major demands made on the Challenger of Record prior to it planning the trials was to place a restriction on the number of competitors to be present and operative in Australia.

Thus, the Costa Smeralda Yacht Club, backed by a majority consensus, introduced the so-called 'performance bond' to facilitate a check on interested associations in terms of seriousness of intention and financial resources. The 'bond' calls for proof of having effected two precautionary bank deposits amounting to $US20 and $US50 million.

As a result, the number of candidates fell from 24 to 14 on the basis of which a calendar of events was worked out for the elimination trials: three round robbins, the first of which is considered as preliminary series, spanning October, November and December 1986 and then the semi-finals and finals to be held in January 1987. Subsequent to the three round robbins a general classification based on a points system is formulated which determines that only the four best yachts go on to compete in the next phase of regattas. The Challenger of Record has already made an important addition to the conditions governing the 1987 races in the form of a clause which will have the effect of imposing a parity on the technical possibilities of both challengers and defenders. Only vessels built and design-tested before September 1986 are admitted to the selection trials. This means that the building of alternative vessels after the start of the races will be strictly prohibited, thus rendering more problematic the copying of an idea which is proving successful for an adversary or the last minute-building of a craft – modelled on another which has been tipped as favourite.

As in the past, each challenger is obliged to participate in the trials with one vessel only but the RPYC, in a review of the situation, eventually conceded that a boat could be substituted after the first round of preliminary regattas but that no points would be carried forward.

The Royal Perth Yacht Club, according to the conditions, is free to enter an unlimited number of vessels in each phase of the trials for the selection of the Cup defender. In this, it is adopting the New York Yacht Club tradition of consistently refusing to discuss its criteria of designation with challenging clubs.

As in the past, the Challenger of Record has laid down that all boats participating in the 1986–87 Louis Vuitton Cup may be modified at the end of each round of regattas. For the first time, however, it has made provision for a fortnight's interval between each round of selection trials precisely so that these modifications can be carried out. Thus, it has been necessary to create two race courses and two race committees, complicating the organizational side still further. Nevertheless, this decision will enable all challengers to carry out any alterations that may be necessary during the four months of racing, some of which are already on the cards, others not.

In the Newport years, the club that traditionally organized the selection trials for challengers was the Ida Lewis Yacht Club which had always left at the disposal of the Challenger of Record its structures, experience and a solid group of enthusiastic volunteers. In 1983, however, the financial involvement of the challengers in the elimination trials was limited to the hiring of one vessel, the cost of which was totally covered by the official sponsor Louis Vuitton.

Since the transfer of the America's Cup to Australia, problems have accumulated and the Yacht Club Costa Smeralda has been forced to take on a greater organizational role, which includes the supervision of 300 races, the establishment of a suitable headquarters, the engagement of committee, press, mark and jury boats and the finding of 60 people willing to transfer themselves on a rotation basis to Western Australia. All this for an event lasting four months. The estimated total cost of preparing the selection trials is about $1,000,000, a budget of significant proportions, covered in large part by the official sponsor Louis Vuitton and, on a smaller scale, by the assignment of television rights and various royalties.

John Bertrand and Alan Bond receive the Louis Vuitton Cup after the 1983 America's Cup.

Match Racing

by Chris Freer

The so-called Olympic Triangle has been designed to test racing yachts on all points of sailing. Yachts race around three buoys, which are arranged in a big triangle producing windward, downwind and across wind (reaching) legs. The course was invented to enable olympic yachts to compete on equal terms at the Olympic Games but it has become the standard course for all top level competition. If the course is used for a race series a simple points score system is used to identify the winner and it has been known for an overall winner not to have won a single race, achieving victory by means of a high average position in the fleet.

Match racing is a sailing joust, normally sailed on the Olympic Triangle. But there are only two competitors and the object is simply to cross the finishing line ahead of one's opponent. There is no second place – something which would have displeased Queen Victoria, whose classic question in search of the salvation of British honour in 1851 was in a sense responsible for the introduction of America's Cup racing. It is the latter event which has become the high altar of match racing.

In order to give the challenging yacht a fair chance for over 100 years The America's Cup has been sailed as a match race. In earlier days the Americans insisted on fleet racing to enable them to smother the challenger, or would substitute defenders tuned to the day's weather. Match racing and the Olympic course have made the racing fairer. Although the Cup represents the ultimate in match racing there are still few helmsmen who can be classed as experts in this specialist discipline. The advent of events like the Congressional Cup in America and its sister series in Lymington, England, have served to publicize match racing as well as giving both organizers and participants more practice. The reality of competition has made helmsmen more competent and has attracted more interest from the sailing fraternity, who recognize the purity of the duel when compared to handicap racing.

As a discipline, match racing requires techniques which are unique in competition sailing. Tactics and the application of the sailing rules must be practised until they become automatic, otherwise the competitor will not even survive the first ten minutes of pre-start manoeuvering. Experience, aggression, quick wits and the grim determination to win are the characteristics of the match racing helmsman. There is nowhere to hide and no second prize.

Out and out speed is not necessarily the central ingredient in a winning boat. Match racing is quite the reverse of fleet racing, where a slow performance can only lead to defeat because of the inability to defend against all the participants. In match racing a cunning and experienced sailor in a slow boat can sometimes use tactics to stay ahead of his opponent, especially if a tactically advantageous position is gained at the starting gun. In 1986, the American defender *Liberty* was slower than *Australia II*, but her helmsman, Dennis Conner, nearly won the series because of his well practised techniques, honed by several thousand hours of trials. There is no doubt that the first battle his adversary faced was psychological due to the sheer reputation of Conner the helmsman.

The sudden elimination which results from a mistake at top levels makes for aggressiveness, but this must be tempered because the penalty for an inadvertant rule infringement is disqualification. The use of the sailing rules to create a condition of physical and mental siege against one's opponent is alien to most yachtsmen who see the rules as citizens view the law: a defence in a law-abiding world. The shock of aggressive boat handling is a revelation to an inexperienced sailor.

It is only in recent years that European sailors have understood the nature of a game which has been an American preserve. Constant reference to the rule book is regarded as unsporting unless the infringement is blatant, whereas 'across-the-pond' sailors are brought up with one hand on the tiller and one on the protest flag. Winning in the protest room is now almost as honourable as victory on the water and the skills of an aggressive IYRU lawyer/sailor receive high praise in today's sharp world. A competitor must also be aware of the slight differences of rule interpretation on each side of the Atlantic, a problem which has tripped up the unwary in the past.

In order to compete at the highest level of match racing the skipper must have the support of a crew whose experience matches his own. The overall skill of the crew must then be built on to produce a psychologically balanced team that works in harmony under stress. The responsibility of the crew in an America's Cup competition is enormous, with three years work and the hopes and ambitions of so many people resting on their shoulders. The skipper plays a big part in welding his 10 fellow crew members into an effective competitive outfit, which can be relied upon at the most crucial moment.

The ten-minute gun heralds the free-for-all; by the five-minute signal concentration is focused on the final sequence of moves which will place the yacht for a perfect start. In a fleet start this is normally at the best end of the line, in clear air with the bow splitting the gunsmoke at maximum speed. Match racing starts can be very different because timing is subservient to tactical advantage. A dominant helmsman attempts to chase his opponent away from the start line without respite, sometimes making for the line many minutes late but with his adversary tucked away astern at some distance. The pirouettes and manoeuvres after the ten-minute signal, as two skilled skippers seek to achieve advantage without fouling each other, are often too complex for the average sailor to follow because of the radical interpretations of the racing rules.

To prevent the fight starting in the harbour mouth, the participants now position themselves at opposite ends of the start line just before the ten-minute signal, having first tossed a coin to decide

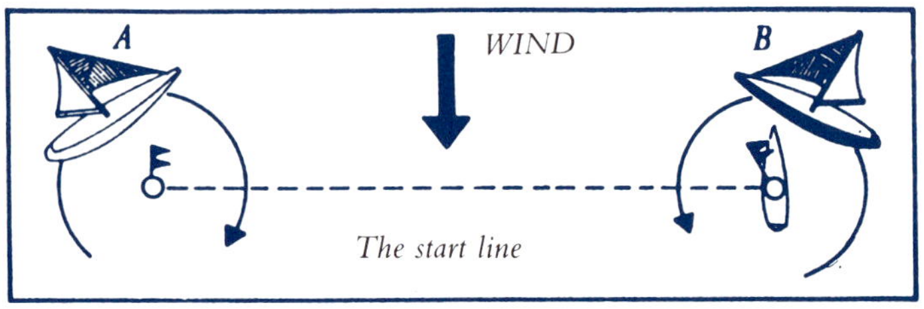

At the ten-minute gun

ends. Tradition demands that the competitors charge, making a hard turn on meeting, in an attempt to secure the tailing position. But some craftier practitioners wait for their adversary to come to them, hoping to capitalize on some error of approach. The favoured close-astern cover is difficult to break, unless the man astern makes a mistake in judging his speed, and can often prevent the boat ahead from tacking or jibing back to the line. The rule is simple: 'a boat that alters course must move away from a boat that is pursuing a course . . .' The pursuer prevents any alteration of course towards the line, maintaining control until it is time to tack and return with the adversary in tow.

One of the approved methods of breaking a cover from astern before the starting gun is to luff slowly head to wind forcing the following boat to do the same. With both boats hanging stalled there is often an opportunity to turn the tables and escape, or even to pick up a controlling position. Lighter, more manoeuverable boats, have a considerable advantage during the start because they are able to turn inside the opposition as well as accelerate or decelerate quickly. This ability can prove decisive in the 'circling' tactic, sometimes mutually set up by the helmsmen. A vicious spin of the boat onto starboard tack as a method of gaining control from this neutral situation, can initiate the favoured tail chase as the opponent breaks away.

The lead boat is perfectly entitled to use obstructions like the committee boat or the spectator fleet as

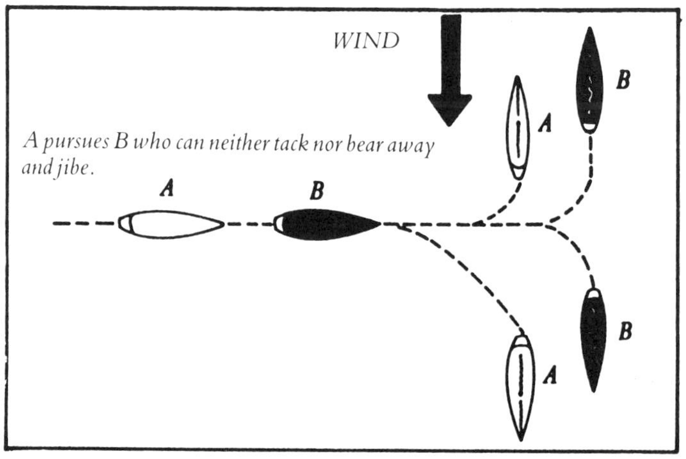

COVERING BEFORE THE START

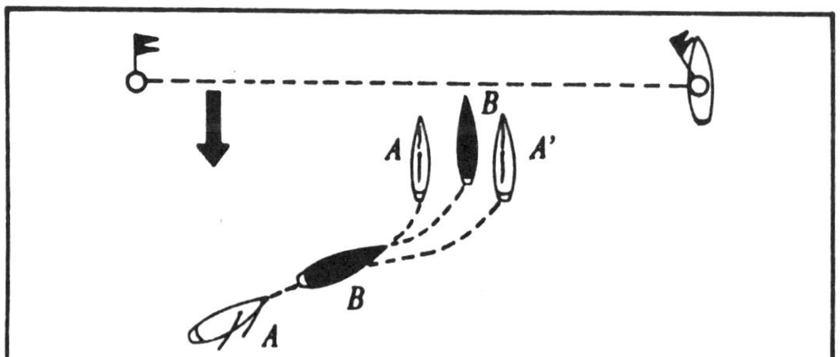

B stops head to wind to avoid being covered. A stops too, either on its opponent's starboard or port side.

BREAKING COVER

part of the tactical play. The hunted boat can orbit the committee boat without risk of being cut off across the circle but care must be taken that the timing of the break for the line is not so early as to risk interference or so late that the opposition starts first. If used close to the starting signal the tactic of circling requires perfect timing.

One of the main problems of 12-Metre yachts concerns their weight and associated lack of acceleration during light weather. During a winding match at the start, the boats can lose the precious momentum which gives the '12s' their advantage with regard to apparent wind. For this reason a good helmsman fights to retain every bit of speed because this adds to the pointing ability of the boat at the start. A poorly timed late jibe has been the downfall of many match racing starts because the boat just dies in its tracks.

Before the ten-minute gun, the tactician, the helmsman and the navigator will have been going through a routine as vital as an aircraft's pre-flight check list. The length of the line will be timed in both directions, the true wind will be checked and then continuously monitored and the relative position of the weather mark noted; tide will be checked as will transits giving a visual check on the start line. The result will be a policy decision on the best starting position.

Generally speaking, if a yacht had the advantage at the start, it should start on the same tack as the other yacht so that the sequence of controlling manoeuvres can be initiated correctly. All of the take-off procedures and attacks have one thing in common: the slow luff to windward and a preference for starting at the committee boat end of the line which necessitates that the boat should be positioned to starboard in any final move toward the line. If the buoy end is favoured then stay to port. The safe leeward start on port tack can be the start of a good control sequence, but an even start to starboard on starboard tack has been shown to give the windward boat an advantage.

The ploy of hanging around the committee boat and sailing slow, hoping to shut the door on the opposition usually comes unstuck because the latter arrives with speed and can choose to go through the gate or swoop to leeward at the last moment. This is a classic following yacht control mechanism but it does require that the line is hit on the gun. With perfect timing the following yacht can pick the right end of the line to go, leaving the other yacht flat-footed.

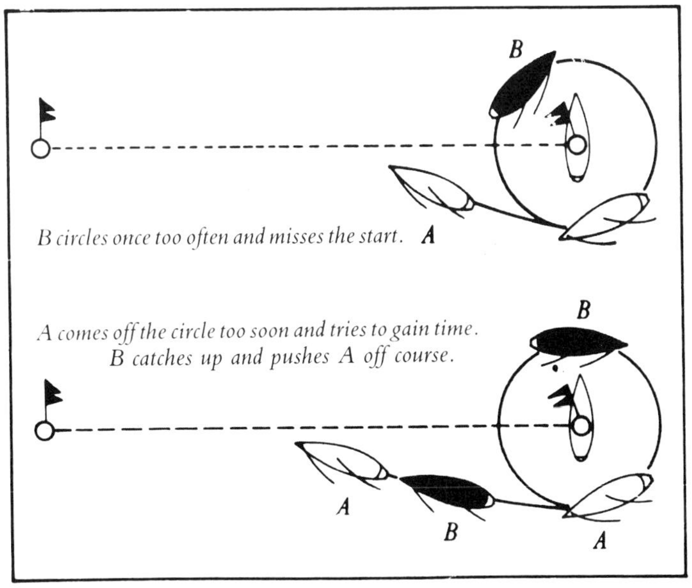

Breaking cover around the committee boat

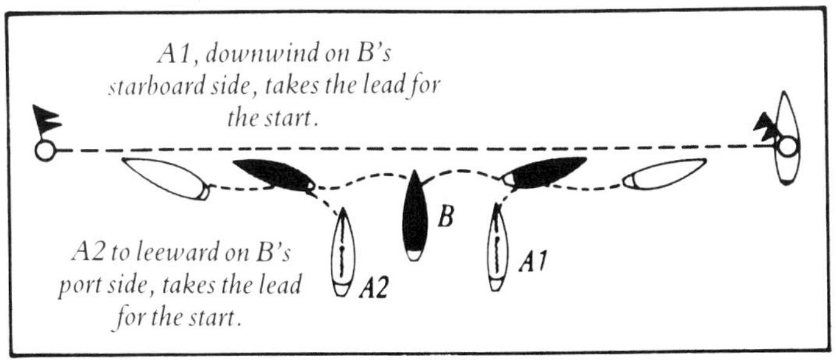

The start

Nowadays, starting manoeuvres frequently result in one or other yacht taking control by means of superior skill. In the past, competitors were often satisfied if the start was even, because there was less aggression and a desire to avoid protests.

Most sports are played within a clearly defined area marked by flags and lines: a match race on an olympic course is no exception but there are also undefined zones, dictated by tactics, in which it is generally wrong to operate. A classic windward course from the starting line will stay within the lay lines of the limits of both tacks. When drawn this produces a lozenge shape, the limits of which are dictated by the pointing ability of the boat. The absolute tactical rule is that one should *never* sail outside this zone on the way to the weather mark.

More often than not, one side of the course is favoured due to wind shifts, but in match racing it is vital to cover one's opponent closely, so the lead boat monitors the advantage, working the wind lifts into its detailed tactics, while maintaining the cover. The boat ahead tries to sail the boat astern to the sides of the lozenge where a tack will initiate a procession to the mark, robbing the latter of any major tactical ploy. The attacking boat seeks to break the sequence of covering tacks and to sail up the lifting side of the triangle bounded by the start line and the weather mark at the apex.

Covering the opposition to windward from ahead entails not only keeping on the same tack, but placing the yacht so that it gives the following boat 'dirty wind'. Dirty wind is the disturbed wake shed downwind from the sails of a boat. It is there on all points of sailing and is a powerful weapon when used properly. The disturbed air is not only full of weak and shifty vortices, but it changes in direction relative to the true wind. A yacht sailing in dirty air can neither achieve speed nor point properly and is therefore forced to tack to clear its wind.

The zone of dirty wind behind a 12-Metre can extend for seven boat lengths astern in an area about 30 degrees abaft the leeward beam. The boat ahead times his tacks so that the second boat falls in this area, thus slowing down the adversary. There are two methods of maintaining control of an opponent. The first is to keep him in the area of dirty wind but the second is more common and demands more skill. This is when an opponent is under the weather bow in clear air or clear astern on more or

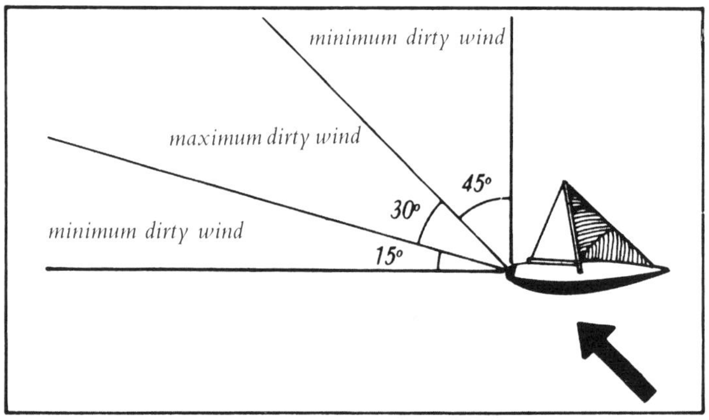

THE AREA OF DIRTY WIND

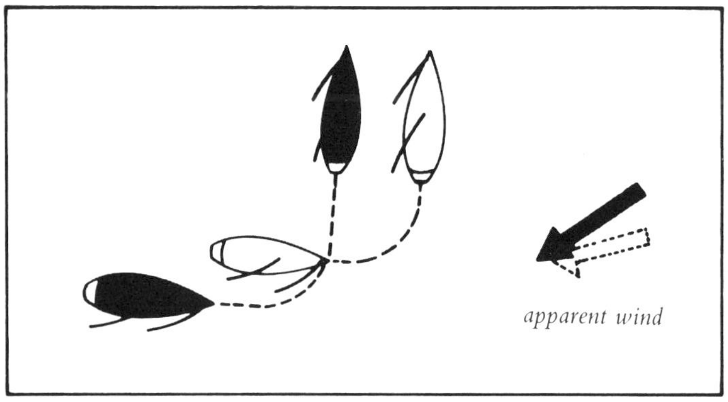

APPARENT WIND

less the same track. In the latter instance only good boat speed and alert covering tacks will keep him at bay.

The technique of staying ahead often involves many tacks, as the attacks are delivered from the trailing boat and countered by the leader. The tactician on the leading boat tries to encourage steady sailing if he thinks that the speed difference is negligible, because in every tack there is a risk of a failure of timing or of equipment. By keeping the pressure on, the attacking boat tries to force some sort of error on the leader.

The attacking yacht will either try to break the cover by sailing faster and higher on the tack on which the boat has the clearest wind or by breaking the sequence of covering tacks. The break can be achieved by timing or simply by false tacking. The latter manoeuvre cannot be used often because its success is due to the element of surprise. In a false tack the attacking boat is put about in the normal way and is held head to wind until the defender is committed to the covering tack, at which point the attacker forces his yacht back onto its original course. At this stage the defender loses some of the initiative because he cannot let the attacker sail off alone in search of a different and maybe favourable wind pattern.

When tacks have been split the attacker tries to get onto the starboard tack and force the defender to tack. As soon as the defender is committed to that tack, the attacker tacks to port to clear his air and hopefully comes further ahead at the next meeting. If he does not make this tack then the lead boat will have a safe leeward position which he will use to squeeze the attacker, eventually forcing a tack which will be covered, so setting up a new control sequence.

All the time the defender watches his opponent like a hawk, playing him off to the side of the course in the hope that he will get a long sail into the weather mark on starboard tack, with the other boat trailing on the lay line. If the attacker is close enough he tries to force the leader to defend himself by tacking all the way to the mark in the hope that he will force an error on rounding with the spinnaker.

The first spinnaker leg is a reach followed by a jib at the wing mark. Tactically, there is little for the lead boat to do except maintain speed by means of some concentrated trimming while the tactician keeps an eye on the trailing yacht. The yacht astern can try to pass to weather but this will be countered by a sharp luffing match. Alternatively, the attacker can try to either establish an overlap at the wing mark, forcing his opponent to give room, or by taking the mark smoothly and wide, sail high fol-

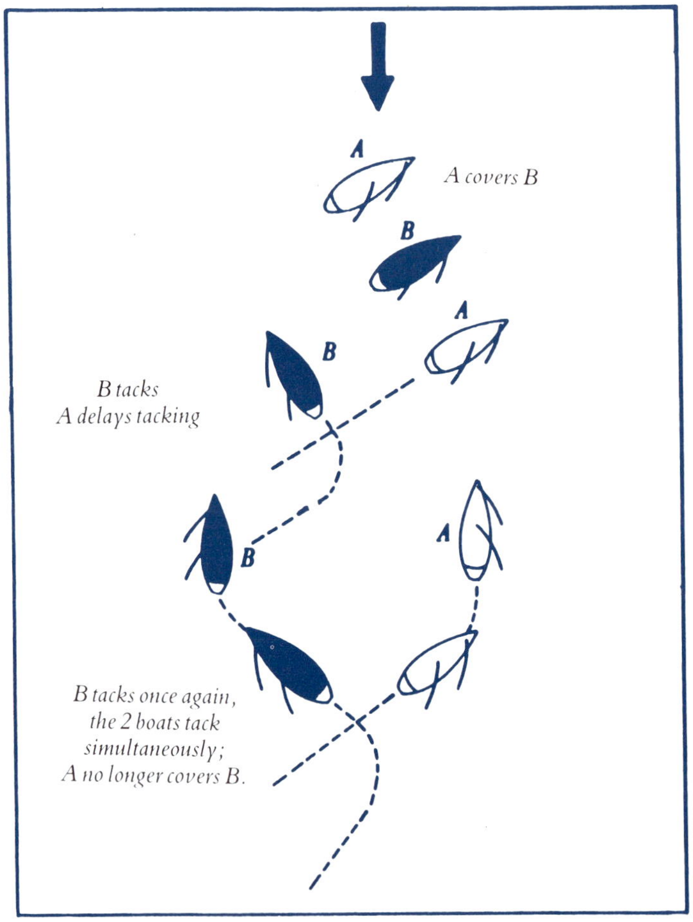

Covering on the upwind leg

lowing the jibe. The latter ploy can sometimes catch the leader in a poor defensive situation especially if his crew have not jibed well.

Very rarely, a leading boat will luff in order to carry the attacker past the buoy but to make this legal he is forced to pass the wrong side of the mark himself. Both boats must then turn and scramble back to the rounding mark. Presumably the leader, being better prepared, will be ahead but this is a risky tactic, even if it is fun for spectators.

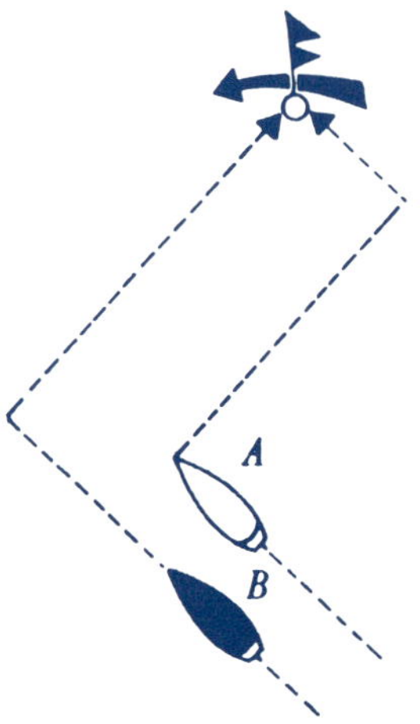

11

A is between 10–15 lengths from the buoy. A leaves its port side covering position and manoeuvres slightly to starboard in order to clear its passage to the buoy in clear conditions. B is also clear but forced to go through a series of slow and delicate manoeuvres in order to get to the buoy. . . . not to be done in changeable winds.

Making for the windward mark

The reaching legs in 12-Metre racing are the least exciting because boats tend to be sailing at a similar speed and there are few skilled moves which the attacker can use to alter his position. On the downwind legs, on the other hand, this changes and even though the boats look pretty and settled on their long run to leeward, woe betide a tactician who relaxes for a second. *Liberty* lost the America's Cup by failing to cover efficiently on the last run.

A yacht must be at least seven lengths ahead at the weather mark to be clear of the attacker's dirty wind. The defender in the lead must keep his wind clear and must place himself between the attacker and the leeward mark. Splitting tacks downwind can be as fatal as it is upwind, with the port and starboard rules creating some fraught situations if the attacker is too close astern. Constant attention to the best Vmg for the conditions is necessary to ensure efficiency.

So, after four beats, two reaches and two downwind legs in a four- or five-hour race you can be lucky to arrive at the finish with an overall lead of one minute or, put another way, about two seconds

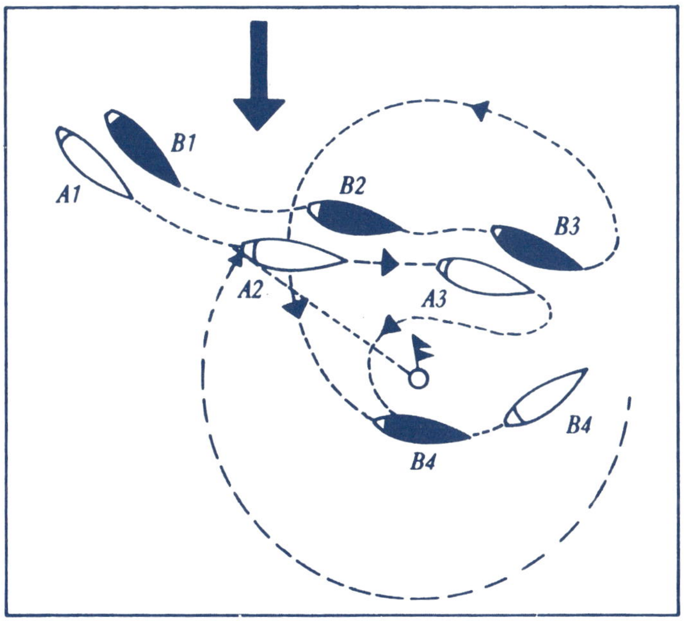

LEADING A BOAT BEYOND THE LEEWARD MARK

per mile. The process is mentally and physically exhausting but eminently satisfying. Of course, the boat must be good but the crew and their combined abilities and willpower provide the essential ingredient, without which the machinery would be an inert gimcrack.

The Sails and Hulls

by John Marshall

Sails are the engines of 12-Metre racing yachts and more efficient, more highly tuned sails convert very simply into more forward thrust to drive the boat through the sea. In addition, good sails produce less undesirable side force which heels the boat over and causes her to slip sideways while trying to fight her way against the wind.

Sail design itself is a challenging pursuit because it blends the need for a sculptor's eye for form and curvature, an aerodynamicist's understanding of the lift and drag produced by wing-like surfaces and a mechanical engineer's grasp of the heavy loads which the thin membrane of sail cloth must carry.

As the America's Cup competition has become more intense, sail design has inevitably become more competitive and demanding. And, as in yacht design, the team approach has become more common. The two sailmaking firms which dominate the competition are both multi-national in their reach and they are fiercely competitive with each other.

North Sails is the world's largest and most successful sailmaker and has the unusual distinction of supplying the majority of the sails for both *Liberty*'s losing effort in 1983 and *Australia II*'s winning inventory. While North's approach to sailmaking and marketing is uncompromisingly technical, the smaller Sobstad company has gained a strong competitive position primarily through the personal approach of its president, Tom Whidden.

Tom started to push his company forward from a group of good second-rank sailmakers when he began to sail regularly with Dennis Conner in 1979. In 1980, he was able to get Dennis to use quite a few of his sails in an otherwise all North inventory. By 1983, Sobstad accounted for 40 per cent of *Liberty*'s racing inventory and Tom is again sticking very close to Dennis, hoping that in 1987 he can push North out of the programme and win the Cup with his product.

Although personalities, friendship and good salesmanship do have a lot to do with how sails get purchased, most of the serious syndicates will spend many hours and hundreds of thousands of dollars conducting objective tests to establish which sails are really fastest.

A 12-Metre sail inventory includes specialized sails for a variety of wind strengths. Typically there are three mainsails and five genoas to cover the full range of conditions from light to heavy wind. In addition, eight spinnakers are required. Several successive designs must be built and tested for each crucial sail in the inventory. At $15,000 to $20,000 per sail the bill can add up very quickly!

The sailmakers will have two critical problems to solve. What is a fast shape for a particular function? How will the sail be engineered to hold that shape under the very heavy loads it will experience?

The computer prediction of 12-Metre sail shape performance goes back at least to 1977 when Heiner Meldner and Tom Schnackenberg developed North Sails' 'flow program' to calculate lift and drag for alternate sail shapes. The computer has helped greatly to narrow the field of inquiry to the most promising shapes, but it has a hard time distinguishing between closely matched sails. The winning edge in 12-Metre racing is very small and elusive. When it comes to sail shape the final arbiter is often the skilled eye. The skipper, the sail trimmer or the sailmaker may be able to identify the subtle differences between good sails and the best sails. Certainly a strength of the *Australia III* programme is Tom Schnackenberg's expertise as a sail designer while Dennis Conner will rely heavily on his own experience and instincts to identify the best sails.

The engineering side of sailmaking is much more analytical and precise than the identification of fast shapes. It starts with the sail cloth itself which must be light, enormously strong and stretch resistant. It seems that each recent America's Cup match has seen a distinct step forward in sailcloth technology. 1977 saw the ultimate development of woven Dacron by Hood and the introduction of Mylar sails by

North. In 1980, Mylar was commonplace and North made the first Kevlar/Mylar composite fabrics. All of *Freedom*'s 1980 racing mains were Kevlar but Kevlar jibs were yet to be perfected. In 1983 everything was Kevlar. Where will we be in 1987?

Sails for Perth will need to be much tougher and more durable than optimal sails for Newport. This is a real problem since Kevlar fatigues quickly in use and old Kevlar sails are prone to failure. North believes the most likely success will come from careful adjustments to the construction of Kevlar fabrics. Their new NorLam fabrics have higher Kevlar content to increase the safety margin. In addition, the material is processed to protect the delicate fibres from the abrasion and flexing which steal its life. The new NorLam Kevlars are 30 to 40 per cent stronger than anything other sailmakers have available.

But is there technology beyond Dupont's Kevlar? Allied Chemical believes their new Spectra fibre may be the answer. They claim it is lighter and stronger than Kevlar and can match Kevlar's remarkable resistance to stretch. A number of sailmakers have tried Spectra sails but so far have met with frustration rather than success.

It seems clear that Spectra is indeed superior in its resistance to fatigue from flexing in use. As a result, there is much less risk of the sudden failures that are all too common with Kevlar sails. But, Spectra, with apparently very low stretch, has an alarming tendency to creep under load. When a sample is initially subject to, say 50 kilos per cm load it may stretch only 10 units on the graph. This would match the low stretch behaviour of Kevlar. But if the load is maintained steadily the material continues to yield! After 120 minutes the stretch may be 15 units and after 30 minutes, 20 units. The result of this insidious continuing stretch is that an initially beautiful sail will quickly distort out of shape and become worthless. Allied has been aware of the problem for some months and is now testing a new formulation, Spectra 1000, which is better but probably still not good enough. Meanwhile, time is running out on the chemists. To advance from the theoretical to the practical in just a few months will be very difficult to do.

The 1987 America's Cup may possibly see the first use of Spectra in mains and genoas. It will definitely be the first Cup in which high-tech laminated fabrics are used for spinnakers, which for years have been made of woven nylon.

The American cloth manufacturer, Dimension, has introduced a new spinnaker cloth made of a film plastic version of Mylar. Because this material becomes more stretchy when it is wet it still needs to be improved but it does look interesting. So far, the most promising materials appear to be North's polyester/Mylar NorLam spinnaker fabrics in weights from 0.8oz for light and medium spinnakers to 2.2oz for real heavy air reachers.

The benefit of the NorLam spinnaker cloth is that the stretch in a NorLam chute is half of that of a nylon chute. In addition, the material has no porosity whatever and does not absorb water. As a result the sail stays light in weight even in very wet conditions.

Sail designers feel that less stretch will be beneficial. But the shift to less elastic fabric involves redesigning the cut of the sail itself. Since the sail will distort less under load, smaller stretch corrections will be required and the actual three-dimensional shape cut into the sail must be fuller and more powerful. In addition, the geometry of the panel curvatures needed to produce the correct moulded shape must be more precise than ever before. Since the fabric will not stretch, it will be quite intolerant of any flaws in the design.

The demand for better design geometry has led to the development of new computer spinnaker cutting programmes. North's 'true radial' spinnakers are entirely computer moulded and can be readily recognized at a distance because they have no horizontal panels – only a radial head, tack and clew. Sobstad is also working very hard on improvements in spinnaker design and has even tested spinnakers with Kevlar reinforcing threads bonded to the cloth.

Since both the upwind sails (mains and genoas) and spinnakers are now all computer designed it makes sense that they also be computer cut. The computer cutting tables are 100ft long so the longest panels on a 12 metre main are easily cut out directly by the computer driven cutting head.

Again, in 1987, an increase in the complexity of panel arrangements will be evident. In 1980, Australia's Tom Schnackenberg turned things upside down by running the panels vertically in the light Mylar genoa. Before long the vertical arrangement had evolved into a radial head and clew joined by a vertical mid-section. Now all three corners are radial and there are, in addition, several horizontal joining seams.

Sobstad's latest sails have, in addition to all the standard structural dazzle, a spider web network of Kevlar straps applied to the sail surface to further distribute the loads and lower distortion.

Sails for 1987 will be an optical tour de force. Golden Kevlar, white Mylar and even pale blue Spectra, will be seen in every imaginable geometric pattern. All in search for a few kilos less total weight or a minute reduction in stretch.

Are the Alan Bonds, the Fritz Jewetts, and the other great patrons of America's Cup racing, the modern day Medicis, sponsoring a Renaissance in yacht design? Until preparations began in earnest for the 1983 match, such an idea would have been too strong. Design was important, but great emphasis was also placed on sails, spars, crew training, and the basic tactics of match racing. All these elements remain important, but after their poor showing in 1980 against the meticulous *Freedom* campaign the Aussies decided they could never beat the Americans at the basics and would have to go for a design breakthrough.

As all the world knows, the Aussies achieved the breakthrough they needed. *Australia II* was an elegant and beautiful solution that took the state-of-the-art into a new era in a single graceful leap. The way the Aussies achieved this leap and the committment of the rest of the world not only to catch up, but to go further still, indeed do mark the dawn of a new period of creative fervor that involves many of the world's finest technical minds, both yacht designers and experts from other disciplines. And, indeed, the costs are high and the great patrons are essential players in the drama of rebirth.

Just how did the Australians do it? First, of course, by committing mentally to the concept that only with a truly superior boat could they win. The American machine had ground up Australian challenges in 1974, 1977, and 1980 with methodical precision and might, but little imagination. Taken on its own terms, the Conner system was intimidating, apparently invulnerable. But in 1980, the Australians stole a great idea from the British and at the last moment installed a super bendy mast that allowed extra sail area to be carried in light air. With it, they won the second race and sparked the idea that better ideas could beat the machine.

Compare the Australians' determination to go forward with the defender's attitudes. In America, the pervasive philosophy was that the 12-Metre design puzzle was essentially solved and only minor evolutionary progress was possible. After all, *Courageous* in 1974 barely, and purely by virtue of being aluminium rather than wood, beat 1967 winner *Intrepid* to become defender. In 1977, *Enterprise* did not show as a clear design advance and *Courageous* won again. In 1980 *Freedom* beat *Courageous* handily over the summer but Conner masterminded a brilliant campaign while Ted Turner never seemed to have his heart in the season's racing. *Freedom* was good, but was she really much faster than *Courageous*?

To the extent that Conner did make an effort to break new ground for 1983, it was done the wrong way. Two designers, Sparkman & Stephens, and Valentijn, were given the assignment of designing new 'radical' boats. They were kept completely independent of one another and, in fact, played off against each other in a competition that alienated both and produced two slow '12s', *Magic* and *Spirit of America*. Without an adequate research budget, without any cooperation between the design firms and without strong interaction or guidance from the experienced sailors in the programme it would have taken great luck for either boat to be a winner.

The Australians did not win by luck. They put together a multi-disciplinary and multi-national creative team, a true twentieth century task force for winning a nineteenth-century trophy. That the nineteenth century rules were perhaps bent a bit in the process was unprovable and ultimately irrelevant to the achievement. The white boat was fast because the Lexcen/Van Oossanen/Sloof team embodied the skills and breadth of experience needed to break out of the trap that says only yacht designers can be involved in designing yachts.

With Bond's enthusiastic support and generous funding, we can imagine the creative sparks flying as key members of the team exchanged ideas, challenged each other to do better or huddled together trying to get a grasp on elusive elements of the design.

Lexcen, the yacht designer and conceptual thinker knew what he wanted: a light, nimble attack boat that could feint and parry, thrust and riposte. She had to fly in light air but how could she also have the power to go in a breeze? Sloof, the aerodynamist could see the implications for better tacking and manoeuvering in winglets but who in the team integrated the difficult and often contrary requirements?

Peter Van Oossanen's computer model for putting all the factors together and predicting the optimal sailing speed in a particular condition, Velocity Prediction Programme or VPP for short, was essential as was his careful tank test methodology.

The Australian model for success was well established in 1982 and 1983. The essential elements are:

1 A team approach with a lead yacht designer and key players from other disciplines.

2 A strong tie with the aerospace industry and the powerful computer programmes the aero people can bring to bear.

3 A strong model test programme to verify both the computer predictions for lift and drag and the intuitive hunches of the designer.

4 A well-developed Velocity Prediction Programme to weigh all the various elements of the design and the test results and read out a performance evaluation.

5 Strong support for the design programme from the syndicate head and plenty of money to carry the technology forward.

Since details of the design methods of the serious contenders are generally secret, it is hard to be sure how each syndicate has advanced from this formula. What is certain is that everyone must accord respect to the Lexcen team approach and to some degree follow his lead.

To take the Conner syndicate as an example, however, there are important differences in style from Lexcen's approach. Our group felt that a potential weakness lay in having a yacht designer, who by personality must be a combination of artist and technician, take overall responsibility for the technical effort. My own background as a scientist by training, an experienced America's Cup sailor with four previous campaigns as a crew member, and as president of a large multi-national sailmaking firm seemed appropriate to our syndicate.

In turn, I felt we would benefit from a cooperative creative environment and asked three of America's top designers, Britton Chance, Bruce Nelson, and Dave Pedrick, to work on the team under a '*ranger*' agreement that will attribute the ultimate design not to an individual but to our team as a whole. This cooperation has worked extremely well and we have by now built two new '12s' and have our final boat, *Stars and Stripes '87*, well under way.

If we are to win we must succeed in two areas. First, we must have a concept which fits the conditions of the Fremantle course perfectly. Since it is often very windy there, there is a natural tendency to assume a long, heavy and powerful boat will have the straight line speed necessary to beat smaller boats.

But other factors must be weighed. True, it is often windy but also there are quite a few moderate days as well, and a big boat can be terribly slow in light air. In addition, the races are match races requiring the ultimate in manoeuverability and acceleration. Again, big boats will be at a disadvantage. The winner will have to resolve the size question with great finesse.

And, at the same time, he must be absolutely at the forefront in the high-tech aspects of the design. There can be no more surprises like the wings of 1983, to instantly render an otherwise thorough and first rate campaign obsolete.

Eliminating the possibility of a surprise can be like buying insurance. A great deal of time and money is spent to put to rest the fear that a concept which initially seems unlikely to work might actually be a winner. More fun is the freedom and support to push the wilder concepts to their limits, to keep trying to make a favourite idea work despite initial setbacks.

No one can say how radical or far-out the designs for 1987 will be. We already know that this enormous burst of enthusiasm, money and competitive zeal has produced several new boats unlike any seen before. We really are experiencing a Renaissance in yacht technology. The intellectual product of this worldwide effort will have an impact for years to come, not only in yacht design, but very likely in surface ship, submarine and aircraft design as well.

THE RATING RULE

12-Metre Class yachts are required to comply with the Rating Rule and Measurement Instructions of the International 12-Metre Class, issued by authority of the IYRU, March 1985.

Yachts competing for the America's Cup shall comply in every respect with the requirements regarding construction, sails and equipment contained in the Deed of Gift and the Interpretive Resolutions applying to national origins of design and building.

The 12-Metre Class of yacht is based on a quotient of the following formula that equals 12 metres, or 39.37 feet.

$$R = \frac{L + 2d - F + \sqrt{SA}}{2.37}$$

- R = Rating (12 metres in this class).
- L = Length of the hull measured approximately 180mm above the waterline. Corrections for girth are applied to this measurement.
- d = The skin girth is measured on the surface of the hull from the deck to a point on the keel about midships. The chain girth (measured at the same place) is the length of line stretched taut from the deck to the same point on the keel. The chain girth is deducted from the skin girth to give the d component.
- SA = Sail area includes the mainsail and the fore triangle bounded by the mast, forestay, and deck.
- F = Freeboard, or height of hull above waterline.
- 2.37 = The mathematical constant.

The Winged Keel

by Ben Lexcen

The superiority of Ben Lexcen's revolutionary winged keel is generally regarded as one of the greatest single factors behind *Australia II*'s historic America's Cup win in 1983. The concept, which at a stroke, made redundant all conventional keel '12s', has forced designers working on the 1987 challenge into an unprecedented search for new and even more exotic variations on the winged keel theme. Here, Lexcen explains the origins of the concept to Bruce Stannard and points towards a host of fascinating new keel ideas for the first Cup defence in Australian waters.

'A lot of people imagine the winged keel concept is something absolutely new. It's not. In fact it's been around for at least as long as I've been tinkering with boats. I remember attaching wings to the bottom of the centreboard on my eighteen footer years ago. The trouble was we had no instruments to tell us if the damned things worked or not. And besides we had to capsize the boat to stick the centreboard in from underneath. That made things kind of messy before we went racing so we didn't bother with them too much. I even tried wings on my skiff rudders but we gave that up too because the wings were terrible weed traps. American designers tried them on '5.5s' but I think they came to the conclusion that they weren't so hot. We've always known about the aerodynamic theory of the end plate and for a long time, of course, we have seen them used on aircraft to stop the tip-vortices spinning off the end of the wings.

When I went to the Netherlands Ship Model Basin to test design ideas for the 1983 Cup challenge I produced the conventional shape of *Challenge 12* fairly quickly. It was fast, very fast, but I wasn't satisfied. I knew that if we were going to win the Cup I had to come up with something very, very different. In all our Cup challenges going right back to 1962, the American defenders were not only better sailed but they also usually featured some kind of technological innovation which made them just that much faster around the track than our boats. At Wageningen there was a constant creative ferment. All sorts of ideas got tossed in and kicked around. The wings grew out of that. I had convinced myself before I went to Holland that wings weren't such a good idea because of the penalties I'd pay in extra wetted surface would be too high. But I knew that the greatest opportunity for some kind of breakthrough lay in keel shapes so I started drawing really weird things and the Dutch guys were very encouraging. I bounced my ideas off them and they either confirmed them or knocked them down. If they sounded half-way reasonable I went away and did the drawings. As for the wings, well we were sitting around discussing all the force we were generating down deep and how the tip would lose *x* per cent of it and there was this spontaneous realization. Why not stick a couple of winglets down there and see what happens. We used computers to calculate the size and shape of the wings.

The first unconventional keel we tested was an inverted one without winglets. I wanted to make the keel very big because I was worried that a small keel might go sideways. It turned out to be way oversized but still the test results showed we were on the right track. We reduced it little by little by trial and error. What we wanted was more lift, less drag. You could put a big lead torpedo on the bottom of the keel but then it becomes a no-lift surface. They're so round they don't generate any lift. You just finish up with a whole pile of wetted surface. We wanted maximum volume in the least amount of area. Anything that pokes out anywhere is a bad deal for wetted surface. But what if we poked some protrusion out of the sides which was flat and didn't generate lift? Then we had to work out whether the increased lift would be sufficient to cancel the increased wetted surface.

The winglets on the Lear Jet were the ones that interested us most because they were handling the tip losses and increasing the performance of those planes way beyond their size. We realized the wings were going to be a big penalty in terms of wetted surface but they did have some added attraction of pulling a lot of weight down low so we had to make them as small as possible and consistent with doing a good job. That's where we used the computer. The wings block the vortex, which is simply water leaking from one side of the keel to the other and moving along so that it spins around. The bottom two feet of any keel do not generate any lift because that is wiped out by water escaping from the high to the low pressure side. Because our inverted keel had a very big lower edge we stood to lose a correspondingly large amount of lift. We realized it would stop the lift better if the wings went right to the front of the keel but then the wetted surface would be a killer. We had to discover how short a chord [the fore and aft measurement] we could have on those wings. *Victory '83* went for dinky little ones while we went for 6 foot long wings on our 12ft keel. We made mathematical models of them, from full-chord to 25 per cent chord in 10 per cent increments and we got a curve. We figured that at 60 per cent of the chord we would get almost the same effect as if it were the full length. We made them as small as we possibly could. The optimum was 60 per cent of the chord.

When it came to calculating the width of the wings, we had to come up with the lowest possible concentration of weight with the minimum surface area but this turned out to be a relatively simple geometrical problem. When it came to determining the best angle for the wings, the technicians at NSMB came up with the idea of putting a shaft through the base of the keel and attaching the wings to the shaft so that they could adjust them up or down two or three degrees. They then put strain gauges on the shaft so that they could measure it bending. After each run in the tank they sent a diver down to adjust the wings up or down half a degree until they found the angle which did not bend the shaft and which meant that the winglets were no longer developing any lift. The net result was that the *Australia II* model made less leeway. A conventional 12-Metre makes three or four degree of leeway whereas *Australia II* makes only two or three degrees. In simple terms this means *Australia II* sails a shorter course. If she goes 100 yards forward, she goes only ten yards sideways. Conventional boats are making maybe 20 yards sideways for every 100 yards they gain. I copped a lot of flak from non-believers when the boat was being built. People just couldn't bring themselves to believe it would work. It was hardly surprising. It doesn't look smooth or sleek. In fact it looks quite odd. But we grew to like it. When we were measuring it up at Cove Haven (near Newport) it just sat there balanced on the keel and that was the first time we could stand back and have a really good look at the whole thing. It really looked good. It looked like a giant Plesiosaur with wonderful rounded flippers.

Now there are all sorts of copies and variations coming out on the 1987 boats and I think that's fantastic. I love the idea of stimulating this kind of thing in design. The first of the English boats has an almost exact copy of *Australia II*'s winged keel. The keels on the first two New Zealand '12s' were very fat, almost bulbous and the wings were also massively thick. The New Zealand keels had a much lower centre of gravity than *Australia II* and that's obviously where they get much of their heavy weather ability. The keel we saw on *Italia* during the world championships in Fremantle looks a lot like *Australia II*'s but without the rounded corners. It's like a computerized diagram, almost pointed at the front. I don't think that's all that smart. The *America II* designers have gone for very long keels with wings straight out the bottom and angled down. They have tried all shapes and sizes bolting them on and off.

We made the keel on *Australia III* not a hell of a lot different from *Australia II* but it does have a lower centre of gravity. The wings aren't square quadrangles. They're long, pointed and eliptical. They are much longer, tip to tip than *Australia II*'s wings and they're not angled down as much. They come out almost flat in an attempt to lower the centre of gravity. I've tried all sorts of weird and wonderful keels for *Australia IV*, some with great big blobs on the bottom, some with wings on the blobs, some without wings. I've come up with something that promises to make *Australia IV* at least four minutes faster around the course in 20 knots of wind than *Australia II*. We are going to go higher and faster. We hope that allows us to build on the edge we had in Newport. I expect a lot of other designers will be trying pretty strange keel shapes as well. They never had the guts to break away from the norm before. Now, *Australia II*'s success has given them the guts, given them the courage to explore. I think that's just great. That's what designers should be all about.'